Dr. Greg's **Dog Dish Diet**

Sensible Nutrition for Your Dog's Health

Greg Martinez, DVM
Illustrated by Caleb Laughlin

RIPARIAN

PRESS

A Division of Knowledge Access Publishing

Dr. Greg's Dog Dish Diet

Publisher's Cataloging-in-Publication data

Martinez, Gregory Scott.
    Dr. Greg's dog dish diet : sensible nutrition for your dog's health / Greg Martinez, DVM ; illustrations by Caleb Laughlin.
    p. cm.
    ISBN 978-0-9841278-0-1
1. Dogs—Diseases—Diet therapy. 2. Dogs—Health. 3. Dogs—Exercise. 4. Obesity in animals. I. Laughlin, Caleb. II. Title.

SF991 D7 2009
636.7/089325—dc22   2009907629

Printed in the United States of America
12 11 10 09   1 2 3 4 5 6 7 8 9

BOOK AND COVER DESIGNS BY REES MAXWELL
COVER PHOTO BY ROSEMARY RIDEOUT

I dedicate this book to Lonna, my wife of more than 30 years. She never has been sure what was in the Tupperware containers in the refrigerator. Also to Sadie, Teddy, Archie, Carly, Maisy, Tucker, Reggie and all the dogs that have needed treatment, kept me company, cheered me up, and showed me their uniqueness and personality. I hope that observing how nutrition affected all of them will help other dogs live healthier lives.

I wish to thank my business partner Dennis Harrigan, DVM, who has skeptically listened to and tolerated my "out of the box" thinking about canine nutrition for years. Thanks too, to Pluis Davern and her Sussex Spaniels' teeth, which showed me that I did not have all the answers and prompted me to ask the questions that led me to write this book. And to Lanny and Liz Brown's itchy Multipoo, Coco, who got better after changing ingredients, which goes to show you that even your good friends know things you don't. And finally, I thank Kendra Bonnett who turned my stream of consciousness ramblings into a book.

Table of Contents

Why I Wrote This Book   **1**

Introduction   **5**
A Tale of Four Dogs ⸳⸳⸳⸳⸳⸳⸳ 5
Vet School Was By the Book ⸳⸳⸳⸳⸳⸳⸳ 11

Chapter 1: Getting To the Source of the Dog Dish Blues   **15**
There's a Wolf in Your House ⸳⸳⸳⸳⸳⸳⸳ 16
Commercial Dog Foods May Be Hurting Your Dog ⸳⸳⸳⸳⸳⸳⸳ 26
One Food Bite's Incredible Journey ⸳⸳⸳⸳⸳⸳⸳ 27
Why Dogs Depend On Us for Food ⸳⸳⸳⸳⸳⸳⸳ 29
What's Wrong with Some Types of Commercial Food and Why ⸳⸳⸳⸳⸳⸳⸳ 32

Chapter 2: Your Dog May Be Telling You It's Time for a Diet Change   **39**
Canine Obesity: A Serious Epidemic ⸳⸳⸳⸳⸳⸳⸳ 40
Canine Skin Issues: Why Sweet-em's Skin Itches ⸳⸳⸳⸳⸳⸳⸳ 46
Abnormal Puking and Pooping: Symptoms Not to Take Lightly ⸳⸳⸳⸳⸳⸳⸳ 47
Is Your Dog Suffering from Allergies? ⸳⸳⸳⸳⸳⸳⸳ 48
How Allergies Develop: The Immune System Fights Back ⸳⸳⸳⸳⸳⸳⸳ 49
Help with Allergies: The Challenge of Tests and Medications ⸳⸳⸳⸳⸳⸳⸳ 50
Fleas, Pollens, Molds and Foods...Oh My ⸳⸳⸳⸳⸳⸳⸳ 52
After Years of Ears... ⸳⸳⸳⸳⸳⸳⸳ 56
Diet and Allergies: The Itch Bag Explained ⸳⸳⸳⸳⸳⸳⸳ 61

Chapter 3: Identifying the Most Nutritional Options   **65**
The Case for Omega Oils and Essential Fatty Acids ⸳⸳⸳⸳⸳⸳⸳ 66
The Great Healthy Teeth and Gums Charade ⸳⸳⸳⸳⸳⸳⸳ 69
`Dem Bones and Other Chews ⸳⸳⸳⸳⸳⸳⸳ 71
Meaty-Wheaty Treats Are Doggie Junk Food ⸳⸳⸳⸳⸳⸳⸳ 74
Making Sense of Nutritional Chart Language ⸳⸳⸳⸳⸳⸳⸳ 77
Inexpensive Commercial Dog Foods...Don't Let Your Dog Pay the Price ⸳⸳⸳⸳⸳⸳⸳ 84
The Case for Canned Food ⸳⸳⸳⸳⸳⸳⸳ 88
Schools of Food...er, Thought ⸳⸳⸳⸳⸳⸳⸳ 89

Chapter 4: Putting Nutrition to Work for Your Dog 99

Island Survival: A Breakdown of Ingredients and Their Nutrients 100

How Many Calories Does Your Dog Need? 106

Nature, Nutrients and Diets: A Comparative Nutritional Chart 112

The Good Doctor's Sage Advice: Making My Case for Fats and Oils 116

10 Rules for Your Dog's Better Health 120

Living the Dream: A Great Past and a Hopeful Future 124

Appendix A: The History of The Pet Food Industry 127

Appendix B: Interpreting Pet Food Labels 133

Why I Wrote This Book

I'm Dr. Greg Martinez and I feed my dogs people food, even though in veterinary school I was taught to use only commercial dog food. In truth, feeding healthful people food to dogs contradicts most everything I was taught. But during the almost 30 years that I've been practicing veterinary medicine, I've increasingly relied on common sense and experience as my best teacher.

I wrote this book because I'm certain that many dogs that are overweight, lame, suffering seizures or that have skin, ear, stomach, bowel or teeth problems will improve if the ingredients in their commercial food are changed and healthful, people-food ingredients are added to their daily diet.

The April 2007 pet food recall was my epiphany. Two things were clear: First, I saw just how dependent on processed, commercial food most pet owners have become. Second, I realized how desperately lost we've become without a prepared diet at hand. When the tainted food was reported, many of my clients panicked; they were afraid to feed their pets commercial diets until they knew the extent of the contamination. At the same time—and this proves just how far from natural, whole food sources we've strayed—most had no idea what to offer their animals in lieu of commercially prepared food.

While the pet-food scare helped clarify the problem for me, I'd actually been thinking about dog diets for some time. Observing my own dogs and my patients revealed two, simple, nutritional truths:

1. *Each and every dog is an individual.* As with people, some dogs have food sensitivities, others have digestive problems, a few have slower (or faster) metabolisms, while most can eat and thrive on almost anything.
2. *Most popular "complete and balanced" commercial dog foods are cookie-cutter diets that do not always allow for individual tolerances.* Not all types of commercial dog food or all ingredients are healthful for all dogs. In fact, it's some of the more common ingredients in commercial diets and treats that are the least well tolerated. And in some cases, they may actually be making our dogs sick.

Because I've seen firsthand how many problems can be cleared up with simple dietary changes, I believe all dog owners need to know more about the types of commercial food available and their ingredients. I want you to come away from this book with:

- A basic understanding of the relationship between your dog's health and his diet.
- A general sense of what to consider when determining if your dog needs a diet change.
- Greater awareness and understanding of what goes into a commercial diet.
- The ability to put that knowledge to good use when you read food labels.
- A plan for feeding your dog that is the best solution for both your dog and your lifestyle.

I feel it is important to give you the tools to improve your dog's health. After 29 years in practice, I can tell you that the number of accidents, broken bones and serious problems is small compared with the cases of itchy skin, irritated bowels, gooey ears and diarrhea. Because I now believe so many of these problems can be traced back to diet, I call these ailments the *Dog Dish Blues*. In fact, originally I thought about making that the title for this book. But because my focus is on using nutrition to help improve your dog's health, I decided on the more positive and proactive title, *Dog Dish Diet: Sensible Nutrition for Your Dog's Health*. Good health really does begin with what we feed our beloved pets.

The good news is that even minor adjustments in diet can take care of many common problems, and if you take my instruction seriously, you can probably dramatically reduce your trips to the vet and save money in the process. A commercial dry or canned (preferred) food with the right ingredients and some healthful additives from your meals, the kitchen pantry or refrigerator can make a big difference in your dog's appearance and general well-being in just a few months.

> *The good news is that even minor adjustments in diet can take care of many common problems, and if you take my instruction seriously, you can probably dramatically reduce your trips to the vet and save money in the process.*

I'm going to start by sharing my personal story with my own animals so you'll understand exactly why I needed to question their diet and how I came to my conclusions. My own dogs and patients showed me that what I'd learned in school didn't always tell the whole story. I'll also share with you the science, medical and nutritional information I relied on to formulate my theories on better canine cuisine. And finally, I'll include plenty of practical advice, dos and don'ts and easy tips you can use. I believe that the more you know, the better you'll be able to make educated choices and smart decisions about feeding. *At the same time, I don't want you to overlook serious health issues. You need to know when it's best to consult your vet. My simple rule of thumb is this: When your dog is clearly suffering and you can't see a simple, obvious cause, check with your vet. Please.*

Dog Dish Diet: Sensible Nutrition for Your Dog's Health is not a collection of recipes for making your own dog food although it is one of the options I discuss. Rather, because I believe that simple nutritional truths are the basis for making healthful feeding choices, I will be sharing my experience as well as giving you some of the practical science behind nutrition so that you are fully equipped to make the right decisions for your dog. Furthermore, I want you to remember that there is no one, simple, right answer. Your dog's individual needs will dictate the choices you make. By reading this book, you'll be better able to understand what your dog requires and how you can best fulfill those needs.

I have dedicated my life to animals, and dogs always have had a special place in my heart. The needless suffering of some dogs due to commercial diets and treats make it necessary for me to share my story with you. Ultimately it is up to us. While we can choose to bear the consequences of our own unhealthful diets, our dogs have to eat what we give them. We can easily make their diet healthier. I think we owe it to them.

Bone Appétit!

Greg Martinez, DVM

Introduction

Veterinarians usually do not pick out or buy their pets. Animals, generally the unwanted, find us. Lonna's and my first dog as a married couple was Sadie, an Australian Shepherd-Lab mix with haunting blue eyes. A very muscular, female weight lifter actually intimidated us into adopting her, but Sadie soon became my constant companion on veterinary calls and evening

runs in the country. At times Lonna accused me of spending too much time with Sadie, referring to her as "the other woman."

A Tale of Four Dogs

Soon after, Teddy the Golden Retriever, Archie the Wire-Haired Terrier, and Carly the three-legged Dalmatian all found us. Teddy's owners wanted him euthanized as a puppy because of his thin, frizzy hair coat, his occasional seizures and his floppy wrists. We saved him, and he went on to carry balls, socks and our underwear around the house.

Carly and Archie share a quiet moment.

Archie was a loyal terrier that a Good Samaritan brought to the hospital after finding him wandering around near a major road with a large wound on his butt. I fixed him up and tried to find his owners, but in a few weeks he came home with me to join the others. After a short time, we discovered that Archie, like Teddy, also had occasional mild seizures.

In fact, it was Teddy that prompted me to question a major concept of my veterinary medical education. I'd noticed a product advertised for joint pain and arthritis in dogs made from green-lipped mussels (Perna canaliculus). In school we were taught that "nutraceuticals" (nutrient + pharmaceutical = nutraceutical) like green-lipped mussel extracts were unlikely to work. Veterinary nutrition courses advised that everything that is eaten is broken down into pieces by digestive processes and sent to all tissues of the body, not just the joints. And yes, you'd think that a small pill or two wouldn't contain enough mussel ingredients to go around and help all the joints in need.

Teddy

Still, Teddy my defective Golden Retriever had bad hips and a bad back that developed in his later years. He needed some pain relief, but in those days the safe, nonsteroidal, anti-inflammatory products we use now weren't available. Too, the aspirin, phenylbutazone, and prednisone anti-inflammatory agents all had side effects when administered long term. Best not to resort to them when there were other options. I had my doubts about the pain-relieving, green-lipped mussel extract, but the product was virtually free of side effects...unless Teddy was allergic to mussels.

Figuring there was nothing to lose, I ordered some, and when the supplement arrived I started Teddy on the suggested dosage. Lonna and I both noticed that in a short time Teddy was in less pain. He improved while we gave the pills and got worse when we stopped them.

That's the beauty of pills and canine patients. There's no placebo effect. Teddy didn't know he was being treated with a product to help his joints, but his joints let him know. I started prescribing the pills for dogs that had the beginnings of arthritis and joint problems and observed similar results. I had no doubt that the active ingredient in the green-lipped mussel extract helped ease joint pain. This was the first time I experienced how nutrition can help heal the body. Since then, 1000s of experiences with glucosamine, chondroitin, MSM, fish oil and healthful ingredients have demonstrated the positive effects good nutrition can have on a dog's life and health.

Carly was an orphaned Dalmatian that suffered irreparable damage to her leg after a run-in with a car. Despite intensive care, one front leg had sustained irreversible circulatory damage from the collision and required amputation. She was a most loving and forgiving patient and accepted treatment without demonstrating animosity or even pain. Unbelievably, after all her surgery and treatments, she still followed me from her kennel to the hospital treatment area. A few days after the amputation, I took her home and told Lonna she needed observation and long-term nursing care. Lonna knew immediately that we had another roomie. In no time at all, we'd added three dogs to keep Sadie company.

Carly's gait looked awkward for a few months after the surgery, but it smoothed out over time. When I thought she was ready, she joined Sadie and me on my daily ranch visits. As one of those visits was to a dairy farm near the ocean, I always took Sadie to the beach for a walk after finishing up. In the beginning, Carly had trouble walking, let alone running, on the sand, but after a few months she was

Sadie taking time to relax and smell the flowers with Carly.

just another crazed dog tearing down the beach after the shore birds. You would have had to look closely at that young, healthy, black-and-white blur to realize she only had three legs.

One day Sadie, Carly and I headed down the beach to the Parajo River. It was low tide, and the river looked shallow. I had planned to carry Sadie across (she was 13, no youngster, and hated to swim) and then return for Carly. When I stepped off the sandy bank, I was in waist-high water and needed to concentrate on my footing and balance. A sudden bump against my body startled me. I was relieved when I discovered the bump was not a shark but Carly, splashing away at my side with an out-of-kilter dog paddle and making fine progress. Her missing limb didn't discourage her; she was simply afraid that Sadie and I would leave her behind.

Carly was responsible for changing the way I feed my dogs. One morning at 5:00 a.m., I received a call to deliver a baby calf. Only hours earlier I'd finished a cesarean section on a Pug, and it seemed as though I'd only just put my head on the pillow. Barefoot and sleepy, I stumbled to the kitchen counter to pour my morning coffee...when I stepped in something squishy. With so many animals in the house, surprises are expected, but you still hate to look. When I did, I saw rejected dog food eaten the night before oozing up between my toes. I had no doubt as to the previous owner of the food. Often after eating her food, Carly would go out in the backyard and graze on grass like a cow and then become nauseous and throw up. With this recent and most undesirable incident, I vowed to get to the root of her problems.

I started with routine screening tests to rule out infections and other medical issues. Carly's blood tests and X-rays were normal except for her missing leg. When blood tests and X-rays do not reveal any issues, veterinarians start dogs with chronic stomach and bowel problems on medication and a hypoallergenic diet. A hypoallergenic diet has ingredients with the lowest probability of causing an allergic reaction. I began feeding Carly dry food (chicken-and-rice kibbles) then switched to Spot's Stew (Halo's natural, commercial food).

Now remember, I had three other dogs at the time. If you only have one pet, I have to explain my challenge: It's almost impossible to feed one dog a special diet and the others something else. It doesn't matter if the new diet is cardboard. The other dogs want it. To make matters worse, the dog on the new diet will try to sneak some of the old food from the other dogs' bowls, negating any benefit. I could either be the food police twice a day or feed all the dogs the same food. Life is just too busy to add food enforcement to the schedule.

So I started giving all four dogs the new, hypoallergenic fare. Lonna had strict orders that the sacred ritual of the nighttime yummy and chew treats also had to be hypoallergenic. We tossed from our cabinets all the allergenic treats and chewy stuff with beef, meat by-products, wheat gluten and corn and found treats with chicken or duck as the protein ingredient and rice or vegetables as the carbohydrate. The dogs don't really need these treats, but as we all know our dogs would think the world had ended if we stopped.

It took only a few weeks for Carly's indigestion to subside. After six months, she only vomited for a good reason...when she ate something dead or sneaked a choice bit of cat poop. She also stopped eating so much grass. I wasn't surprised that a hypoallergenic diet cured the symptoms of indigestion; it was right out of the vet rulebook. I was surprised, however, to observe the effect on the other dogs. With the new diet, both Archie's and Teddy's occasional mild seizures stopped.

Did this hypoallergenic diet stop Teddy's and Archie's seizures? According to the vet rulebook, trauma, infections, autoimmune problems or tumors caused seizures, not diet. I also knew that almost all seizures are classified as epileptic (of, relating to or associated with epilepsy) and mostly idiopathic (having no known cause). I had some pondering to do. My scientific background taught me not to jump to conclusions. I would have to wait to draw any conclusions about food and seizures. But it was certainly food for thought.

Within several months, Archie started having occasional seizures again—mild (petite mal) seizures that occurred once a month or so and would make him wobble and appear dizzy. So much for the food-causing-seizures theory, I thought. But a week later I heard the pitter pat of his little paws coming from the study where we kept bowls of dry cat food. I realized then that he'd been sneaking cat food, eating it along with the hypoallergenic diet. I checked the cat food to see if it contained beef, meat by-products, corn or wheat gluten. Sure enough, the label revealed wheat gluten. I decided then and there that our cats would also have to eat hypoallergenic food and that I'd try to keep the cat food out of the dog's reach. In about two months, Archie's seizures stopped once again. This homespun experiment was good enough for me. That's when I knew nutrition must play a bigger role in health and sickness than I was taught.

> "...a tablespoonful of olive oil or canola oil on the food daily, or an egg yolk in the food three or four times a week, can have a wondrous effect on health."

Today I am a believer. I know that simple acts like changing ingredients, putting a tablespoonful of olive oil or canola oil on the food daily, or an egg yolk in the food three or four times a week, can have a wondrous effect on health. When I take my fish-oil capsules, I always share them with my dogs. I hope that in the course of reading this book you too will become a convert. So to get you started rethinking your dog's diet, I'll ask you: Do you ever throw out leftovers or scraps of poultry, pork, fish, vegetables or potatoes? Next time throw them in the direction of your dogs' bowl. Healthful leftovers are very nutritious, and they add variety to the diet.

Vet School Was By the Book

Like most veterinarians, I came out of school convinced that canine nutritional experts had dog food diets all figured out. My nutrition classes included a very detailed study of the anatomy, physiology and different digestive processes of domestic species. We spent a great deal of time on nutritional deficiencies, starvation, diabetes and the functions of the hormones and enzymes involved in the digestion and absorption of food and nutrients. We studied the research, formulas and charts generated by the major dog food companies.

We were taught the nutritional language of charts, ingredients and percentages—the focus of almost all medical-nutrition courses. We did not discuss the reasons for feeding or not feeding our dogs certain types of meat or grain. We were told that the body needs certain percentages of proteins, carbohydrates and fats without regard to the source of the ingredients.

In courses emphasizing the physiology of digestion and absorption, we learned how food is broken down into pieces small enough to cross over from the intestines into the bloodstream, and how the absorbed, floating, food particles flow to the liver where they become building blocks the body can use. Ingested chicken protein, for example, becomes dog protein through amino-acid rearrangement in the dog's hard-working liver, rendering the newly manufactured protein available for the body's maintenance and repair.

In my medical-nutrition education, the emphasis was more on nutritional deficiencies and digestive disorders than on how different

Help Your Dogs Regain Excellent Health

Watch television or read a magazine, and you're sure to see an ad or story promoting our health by eating differently. When it comes to improving people's diets, the specifics vary and the recommendations can range from supplements to dark chocolate (Note: while dark chocolate is good for us, never feed chocolate to your dog.) to vegetarian and raw diets. There is also a general consensus that smaller portions and fewer processed foods are infinitely better for the body than the mix of ingredients in fast food, chips, sweets and soft drinks. A balanced diet contains sane portions and a mix of the water, carbohydrates, proteins, fats and oils from natural foods like meat, fish, vegetables, nuts and fruit needed to maintain, repair and fuel our bodies. My nutritional advice for your dog follows the advice of nutritionists for humans.

Further, I believe that it is not always possible to depend on one complete-and-balanced diet for all dogs' nutritional needs. Just as you wouldn't thrive if you consumed the same meal, with the same ingredients, for months or years on end, so too your dog will probably do better eating a mix of health-enhancing ingredients. Using a good commercial dog food as a base, then supplementing with healthful people food may be the best dog food diet, one that should help your dogs recover from or avoid those dreaded skin, ear, stomach and bowel problems I call the *Dog Dish Blues*. The right type of diet and kind of ingredients can help with chronic health problems, improve the hair coat and will even help your dog lose weight.

ingredients in the diet might prevent conditions. Preventative medicine wasn't something we were taught at the time. We were told, however, that the feeding of homemade diets and scraps was frowned upon because doing so might affect the delicate balance of nutrients and cause medical problems. Nutritional literature and my veterinary education suggested that the formulation of dog food was precise, not to be tampered with. I was taught that most "complete and balanced" commercial dog foods are good for all dogs, and that those diets with their high percentages of grains, meat and meat by-products were nutritionally adequate and would prevent deficiencies. We were led to believe we could advise our clients to open a bag or can of good, quality dog food and put some in a bowl for good health.

I thought I was satisfied with my veterinary nutritional education. However, 29 years of experience with my dog patients and my own pets has taught me that a simplistic, one-formula-fits-all approach may not always be correct. My re-education was gradual at first, but little by little I began to question the basic concepts of what we feed our dogs and why. At first I had more questions than answers:

- *Which kind of meat or grain is healthier?*
- *What's better...canned or dry dog food?*
- *Does a high-carbohydrate, baked kibble contain all the nutrition needed for good health?*
- *How does one know what mixture of ingredients is best for our canine companions, and where is this formula found?*
- *What ingredients should I look for on the label of bags and cans of commercial food?*
- *If nutrition has to be as precise as the dog food companies suggest, can we even be trusted to feed our dogs or, for that matter, our own families?*

After much reflection and study, I came to understand some simple nutritional truths about feeding dogs that, when applied, are neither expensive or time consuming and offer spectacular results.

These truths came from considering the ingredient mix in the diets of our dogs' ancestors and comparing it with current combinations of ingredients in commercial diets—formulas that were developed for the sake of convenience and cost-effectiveness. Some dogs, like some people, seem to be able to eat anything and stay healthy, but at least 30 percent to 40 percent of the dog population requires different ingredients and types of food for optimum health.

The ancestors of our pets evolved eating a diet that worked well for them. I asked myself, how do the ingredients in that ancestral diet compare with today's commercial offerings? And how do we know what types of foods or ingredients are best? This became my quest.

> *...at least 30 percent to 40 percent of the dog population requires different ingredients and types of food for optimum health.*

What I have come to know is that feeding a healthful diet will help prevent many of the common veterinary issues I deal with daily. Not only does a better diet make your dog healthier and happier, a healthful mix of ingredients can often reduce the need for costly diagnosis, medical care and veterinary treatment.

Chapter One

Getting To the Source of the Dog Dish Blues

*I*n my zoology classes, I learned that animals evolved along with their food source. This means that across the millennia their digestive systems became progressively more efficient at processing the food sources around them. In other words, the eater was in tune with the eaten. It makes sense that the ancestors of the dog evolved to efficiently digest the food available to them, and it's reasonable to assume that present-day dogs might thrive consuming much the same mix of ingredients that kept their ancestors healthy. It follows too that the diet of the ancestor of the dog could provide clues to the best mix of ingredients for our pets.

There's a Wolf in Your House

The wonderful roadmap of genetics points to the wolf as being the dog's most likely ancestor: 99.8 percent of your dog's DNA matches that of the wolf. This means your dog's genes only differ by 0.2 percent from wolves' genes. If your dog is a Husky, Malamute or Shepherd, this might seem plausible and even probable to you. If you're sitting next to a toy breed such as a Lhasa, Pomeranian or Pekingese, it's harder to believe. But believe it or not, even the loveable, bug-eyed Pug is a descendant of the wolf. Intense selective breeding has resulted in

> *The wonderful roadmap of genetics points to the wolf as being the dog's most likely ancestor: 99.8% of your dog's DNA matches that of the wolf.*

body types and personalities vastly different from the original wolf model. If you take a moment to think about all the different sizes, colors and personalities of dogs, you have to agree that breeding has introduced some pretty amazing changes. Nevertheless, dogs from the Chihuahua to the Great Dane are more than 99 percent genetically identical to the wolf.

The process began tens of thousands of years ago. In fact, archeological evidence suggests that humans and canines have lived together symbiotically for somewhere between 10,000 years and 25,000 years. To understand how our ancestors tamed the fierce predator that undoubtedly looked a great deal like our modern-day wolf and started the transformation from wild wolf to domesticated house pet, we have to venture into the past and blend fact with a little supposition.

Imagine that you're a member of a small village somewhere on the Euro-Asian continent 15,000 years ago. Your village stays alive by tracking and hunting game and gathering whatever plants, roots, nuts, grains or fruits are ripe and available. One evening after a successful hunt, you and the rest of the village are relaxing and enjoying some hard-earned antelope cooked over the campfire. You finish stripping the meat from a rib and toss the bone toward the garbage pile out in the distance. As you watch the bone arc away, you're suddenly startled by the sound of snapping jaws; at just the same moment you catch sight of a pair of glowing, red eyes reflecting the campfire light. You freeze and watch as a wolf grabs the bone on the fly and vanishes into the darkness.

The next morning, you go to a nearby stream to get water. As you cross the shallow, rocky narrows to the gathering pool, you hear whimpering coming from behind a rocky outcropping. Cautiously you approach and notice a log. The sound seems to emanate from the log, but looking closer you catch the glistening, light-brown eyes of a wolf pup, painfully thin and too weak to stand. The little male pup does not resist as you bundle him up and take him back to the village. After receiving gentle care and good food he becomes stronger and grows accustomed to people. He now thinks that you, your family and the other villagers are his pack. Wolves are, after all, intelligent, social animals that cooperate to hunt, protect their pack and raise their young. The pup transfers this instinctual behavior to his new human pack and insists on being your shadow, watching everything you do and noting when you do it. This is how young wolves learn a daily routine from their pack in the wild, and this wolf pup applies that instinct to his new family.

"Cousin Strider really looks fat since he domesticated."
"Yeah, well, you are what you eat!"

One day while walking with your pet wolf by the stream to gather some ripe blackberries, a startled rabbit bolts across your path. The now strong, young wolf takes chase and runs it down. After coaxing and pulling, your wolf lets you take the carcass. (Not even all dogs will allow this, as you know.) You dress and skin the rabbit and give the wolf some of the organs and the bruised neck muscle. You bring the rabbit back to the village and recount how the wolf made the kill and allowed you to take the rabbit from him. In time, your pet wolf earns his keep by also being the village alarm. He's an adept protector from predators and invaders as well as a hunting partner. The wolf's presence in the village helps fellow villagers realize how valuable a partnership with wolves can be. They are less afraid of wolves and, at the same time, wolves seem more comfortable with the village, seeing one of their kind there. This is one theory of domestication

Another gives our ancestors' trash heaps a lot of credit for the wolf's taming. The consistent, convenient piles of edible garbage near ancient villages could have lured wolf packs to build their dens closer to humans. Eventually, natural selection would favor wolves that were tamer and more tolerant of humans. Wolves with these characteristics would remain closer and get the best leavings. These wolves were good candidates for feeding and domestication.

Regardless how the partnership between wolves and humans began, in the course of generations, wolves or dog-like wolves became the domesticated friends we have in our houses today. This partnership may have improved the odds of survival for both man and wolf during tough times by combining their skills and increasing the chances of a kill. The keen senses of the wolf might have helped our ancestors get close enough to prey to use their spears and knives. Those same keen senses gave advance warning and defense against invaders and dangerous predators.

Wolves and humans co-evolved together across thousands of years, resulting in the tight partnership we have today. In addition to our pets, many dogs work with us as herders, rescuers and guards. That connection is particularly apparent within a number of societies. Take, for example, the symbiotic relationship between the Inuit people and their sled dogs. These dogs provide transportation and guard against polar bear attacks while the Inuit fish and hunt. The dogs are rewarded with seal blubber and companionship. Without dogs, this way of life would not have been possible for the native Inuit all these years.

We care about the origins and ancestral diet of our pets because the study of zoology and evolution teach us that the types of prey and other food that our dogs' ancestors consumed for millions of years may have been the best fit not only for their metabolism but

The Evolution of Dog Food

To understand why we have all these different choices of canine cuisine, it helps to review the evolution of dog food. For a great long time, humans and wolves have been neighbors, sharing the same territory and food. After several thousand years of hunting and gathering, the development of agriculture, and an organized social system allowed our ancestors to stay in one place, put in gardens and grow crops instead of following migrating animals around and finding seasonal sustenance. The bounty of meat and grain from agricultural methods freed man and dog from their hunting chores.

Domesticated dogs needed new jobs. Our ancestors, having discovered that dogs were intelligent, social and adaptable, found them capable of taking on many other tasks. Using dogs for all kinds of different chores became popular, and the number of domesticated dogs increased around the world. Our domesticated dogs with new jobs and new styles became dependent on us for their food and care.

At first, the diets of domesticated dogs consisted of leftovers or scraps, but choices became more diverse as farming methods improved. Meats and grains not used for human **(cont.)**

for that of their descendents today. The theory of natural selection, commonly known as "survival of the fittest," dictates that the animal making better use of its environment and food sources will be more successful than the competition. The strongest, fittest animals will win the eating, dating and mating contests. Since eating, digesting and absorbing food is critical to an animal's success both with breeding and staying fit, the natural diet of our dogs' ancestors may hold clues for the most beneficial mix of ingredients in today's dog food.

We can start by learning what wolves ate in the wild. Studies of wolf

Deer and caribou are part of the natural diet of our dogs' ancestors and their closest modern relatives, wolves.
Photo is courtesy of Wolf Howl Animal Preserve LLC and its licensors (www.everythingwolf.com).

behavior in nature give us a general idea of the ingredients wolves ingest in their natural habitat. Wolves consume large ungulates such as caribou and deer but also eat rodents, birds, reptiles, fruit and berries when the opportunity arises. And when times are tough, they even scavenge off disgusting stuff such as rotting carcasses and poop.

The Evolution of Dog Food (cont.)

consumption were now available for dog food. As the popularity of dogs as working partners and house pets increased, a business opportunity appeared…and dog food was born. Now that working, ranch and family dogs were valued members of a team, commercial dog food found an economic niche by providing a consistent, convenient and supposedly balanced diet for them. Almost all commercial diets available today evolved from processing surplus and cost-effective foods not destined for our tables.

About now you're probably thinking that commercial dog food doesn't compare very well with caribou and worrying about how you're going to get that carcass into the freezer. I've got good news. To feed our dogs well on a diet that resembles the natural diet of a wolf, we only need to make sure the mix of ingredients and nutrients is similar. Picture a caribou, salmon or beaver, for that matter, with a nutrient analysis label glued to its side. You'll also have to imagine yourself close enough to the caribou so you can read it. The analysis would show the

> "To feed our dogs well on a diet that resembles the natural diet of a wolf, we only need to make sure the mix of ingredients and nutrients are similar."

amounts and percentages of water, protein, fat and carbohydrate contained in the natural diet. If this is the mix of nutrients that the ancestor of our domestic dogs evolved to eat, it's reasonable that we should try to make the nutrient analysis of today's commercial diets comparable.

The wild game analysis would show higher amounts of water, protein and fat and a much lower amount of carbohydrate than most commercial dog food offerings (the only exceptions being some of the new grain-free, meat-based foods like EVO). I believe this deviation from the ingredients and nutrients in a natural diet is significant for 30 percent to 40 percent of our dogs and is having a profound effect on

Feed Your Dog's Inner Wolf

Wild Game provides the wolf with a high-water, low-carbohydrate diet that is also high in protein and fat. With the exception of a few of the newer, grain-free, commercial foods, most kibbles are poor imitators of the natural diet; canned dog foods most closely match the wolf's natural diet.

Wild Game (natural diet)
Ingredients:
60-70% Water
40-60% Protein
30-40% Fat
<10% Carbohydrates

Canned Dog Foods
Ingredients:
60-80% Water
20-40% Protein
15-25% Fat
30-45% Carbohydrates

The water percentage is measured separately and serves to show what percentage of the whole food is comprised of protein, fat and carbohydrates. The more water, the smaller the percentage of protein/fat/carbohydrate ingredients in the whole food.

their health. I also believe that ALL dogs will benefit from our efforts to mimic the nutrient analysis of the wild game as closely as possible. *In short, we should feed each and every dog's inner wolf.* And so the quest begins for the commercial dog foods that offer a nutrient mix similar to the traditional wolf diet.

Most percentages are given in ranges as actual numbers can vary by brand. These numbers are meant for very rough comparison purposes only. Notice the big differences in nutrients between the Dry Food, Kibble & Treats category and other food sources. Minerals and ash make up a small percentage of ingredient totals but have not been listed here.

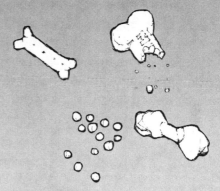

Vegetables*
Ingredients:
80-90% Water
10% Protein
1% Fat (polyunsaturated)
70-80% Carbohydrates

Dry Food, Kibble & Treats
Ingredients:
10-15% Water
15-40% Protein
5-15% Fat
40-70% Carbohydrates

While the wolf doesn't eat vegetables, carbohydrates (primarily in the form of grasses and grains ingested by prey) are part of the wolf's diet. Canned foods include vegetables, and I recommend supplementing every dog's diet with fresh, canned or frozen vegetables to provide needed essential fatty acids, vitamins, and minerals.

A Note About Purebreds

Ever wonder how so many types of dogs, what we call *purebreds*, evolved from wolves and the first domesticated dogs? In the thousands of years since the first taming, people all over the world bred dogs for traits that were helpful or decorative. Dogs were trained to hunt, pull sleds, herd, retrieve and protect livestock (e.g., Pointers, Huskies, Heelers, Labs and Sheepdogs). Or, they were trained to guard, protect or defend (e.g., German Shepherds, Rottweilers, Pit Bulls, Terriers, Mastiffs and Bulldogs). People also bred for small decorative housedogs or varmint killers. The toys had beautiful coats and color patterns and were small enough to adorn palaces, carriages and homes. They also could get into tight places to control rats and other varmints.

Queen Victoria received a *Pekingese* bred by Chinese Buddhists, and soon everyone of that era wanted a small housedog. The great variety of breeds we have from all parts of the world show how popular and widely practiced dog breeding has been. I love the personality and bug-eyed cuteness of the Boston terrier, but compared to their ancestors, they are much different. It's hard to imagine some of our domestic purebreds surviving in the wild. Picture a Pekingese having to hunt and catch its own meals. We have bred the wildness out of the wolf and opted for tameness, size, shape, color and personalities that help us or amuse us.

The sizes, shapes, colors and personalities of the different breeds arise from intense selection pressure for a desired look or trait. The hidden cost of this selection pressure is the corruption of a genetic code that was in harmony with its environment. When we select for flat-face dogs such as *Pugs* and *Bulldogs*, the soft palate, tongue and larynx are crowded in the back of the throat; as a result many of these breeds snore or have breathing problems. Many Bulldogs are also very sensitive to allergenic ingredients in food. Intense selection then has produced a very interesting-looking, lovable dog with breathing problems, skin and ear problems and bowel problems. **(cont.)**

A Note About Purebreds (cont.)

One *Jack Russell Terrier* owner described the breed as a Jack Russell terrorist or "like a gun without a safety." These super active, territorial and aggressive and frequently neurotic dogs are often allergic to pollens, molds, grasses and the allergenic ingredients of dog food. Lonna's sister, Vicki, has a Jack Russell named Lucy that gets so jealous and stirred up when barking at outside dogs that she loses her mind and attacks her housemates in her territorial frenzy. Working with behaviorists or even employing drug therapy such as Prozac may work for some neurotic, anxiety-challenged dogs.

The Jack Russell's temperament is the result of breeding. They were bred for varmint control; they had to be aggressive, quick and fearless. The problem is this pent-up energy and anxiety is often inappropriately expressed when around other living things. They have a bad reputation for demonstrating the precise personality traits that we selected.

Cocker Spaniels, German Shepherds, Labs and *Goldens* are a few of the breeds known to have more ear, skin and bowel problems. They are generally more susceptible and experience more issues with flea, pollen and food allergies. These same dogs also are affected by idiopathic (cause unknown) seizures. I can't help but wonder if selective breeding has made some breeds more sensitive to allergens and seizures. Could these two symptoms be genetically linked? I wonder.

Selective breeding has certainly changed the domestic dog. Intensive breeding for body type, skin color, hair coat and personality has crossed wires in the immune system of various breeds, making them more sensitive to dietary and environmental allergens as well as prone to dry skin, hotspots, ear problems, nausea, diarrhea, anal gland problems and colitis. In my practice, I regularly see Cocker Spaniels, Labradors, Golden Retrievers, Boxers, Bulldogs, Mastiffs, Char Peis, Poodles, German Shepherds, Jack Russell Terriers, Rottweilers, Pit Bulls and West Highland Terriers suffering from a host of allergies. The good news is that healthful changes and additions to their diets can help many of these symptoms.

Commercial Dog Foods May Be Hurting Your Dog

Every day in households across America, dog owners are feeding high-carbohydrate, allergenic diets and treats that may be causing or contributing to common health problems in our canine friends. The majority of these commercial dog foods contain one or more of the allergenic ingredients wheat, beef or corn, and this steady current of inflammatory products is causing many chronic medical problems in susceptible individuals. It wasn't always this way.

The ancient ancestor of our domestic dog ate ingredients that were available in the surrounding environment, including prey and other seasonal or opportunistic food. The very first domesticated dogs undoubtedly hunted some of the same game, while keeping an eye on their human companions for the discarded remains of a hunt, leftover food and even garbage. During the early 1900s, dogs' diets changed as the pet food industry packed and promoted surplus meat and grain products to the descendants of those early canines. These commercial products have made feeding our dogs easy and economical. And because they've been promoted as nutritious, balanced diets, we've felt good about the choice.

Like millions of other dog owners, I assumed that all you had to do was pick a product off the shelf that matched the age, weight, breed or medical condition of your dog. I too was seduced by the sleek Golden Retrievers in the television ads dashing across the screen to bowls filled with "complete and balanced nutrition." It may be possible that those beautiful specimens of the dog kingdom are actually thriving on the advertised brand of dog food; we'll never know. I do know that a television ad portraying an itchy Lab with red, inflamed ears, a German Shepherd so heavy it can barely get up or a Poodle with colitis and blood in the stool wouldn't sell much dog food.

Let's face it. Pretty dogs and attractive packaging move a lot of product in this $25-billion-a-year industry. Alas, what you see pictured on the outside is not always what you get on the inside. As we continue to compare commercial food with the original natural diet (specifically, its mix of ingredients and its percentages of the nutrients) and as we identify the allergenic ingredients in some commercial diets, we begin to realize that commercial foods may not be the best choices for all dogs.

Providing your dog with a healthful diet will require that you review and comprehend all the alien-sounding, nutritional jargon printed on dog food labels. But don't worry; it's not hard, once you know what to look for. In Chapter 3, I'll give you a crash course in label reading because I want you to have the confidence to take positive steps. I've changed my dogs' diet and the diets of 1000s of patients, and most have benefited and none have been harmed from my simple, practical nutritional advice.

One Food Bite's Incredible Journey

We've all heard the saying, "You are what you eat." And we are. A bite of chicken will eventually become you...given a few days. Our food provides the raw material we need to replenish, grow and rebuild our bodies. To give you a better understanding of how chicken (or any protein) transforms into skin, muscle, liver (to arbitrarily name a few body parts), we'll follow a bite of chicken. It's an incredible journey:

The bite-size piece is chewed and ground by the sharp and flat areas of the teeth into small pieces that the digestive juices from our saliva begin to break down into yet smaller pieces. When swallowed, the chewed-up wad of chicken travels down the esophagus to the stomach for an acid bath. Hydrochloric acid, to be specific, further breaks down the protein, while the muscular walls of the stomach work like a washing machine on the delicate cycle to churn the bits and pieces of chicken into a mash. This mash is then pushed out of the stomach and into the small intestine. There, the pancreas and gall bladder in concert squirt digestive juices into the small intestine via the common bile duct to break down the chicken mash into their smallest food particles—molecules.

These molecules, with names such as protein, fat, triglycerides, amino acids, glycogen and glucose, are ready to be brought across the intestinal lining to the bloodstream. They enter the body through special cells in the intestinal lining that guide the molecules through to the blood vessels that flow into the liver. Once in the hepatic cells of the liver, the molecules from that original bite of chicken are added to and rearranged to produce (as in the case of this example) human or dog protein.

This orchestra of organ cooperation needed to nourish our bodies developed in the span of millions of years as humans, dogs, indeed all mammals evolved with their food sources. Their bodies adapted to break down the available edible animal, insect, fruit and plant foods into the tiny building blocks that are necessary to nourish, maintain and repair the body. Since most animals, insects, fruit and plants contain more water and fewer carbohydrates than the calorie-dense, dry diet we frequently eat (pizza, chips and cookies for humans; kibble, biscuits and treats for dogs) it is a wonder our digestive systems have adapted to our new diet at all.

Considering America's state of health, maybe our bodies are waving the white flag.

This book is about dog nutrition, but I thought I could make an important point by illustrating the identical, human-digestive process and the link between the dry, high-carb diet and a host of health problems—obesity, diabetes, joint issues, seizures, to name a few—occurring in both dogs and people. If you or your dog suffer from health problems, dietary changes often can be the best and easiest solution.

Why Dogs Depend On Us for Food

With domestication, *canis lupus* (wolf) became *canis lupus familiaris*—the dog, a creature dependent on us for its food and care. Your dog no longer needs its big canine teeth for hooking prey or defending itself. Neither does it use its sharp, shearing premolars for tearing and crunching muscle, flesh and bone. Those powerful instruments and weapons are now relegated to chewing kibble, canned food, treats and scraps.

Dogs today rely on us to provide the right mix of ingredients to keep them in good shape. Of course, all dogs will occasionally consume objects on their own. Based on some of the patients I've seen come through our hospital, I know they are capable of eating garbage, poop, wood, birdseed, plastic, foil, rubber bands, baseball caps, nine one-pound fishing weights, a client's underwear and any of several dead disgusting things. Even with all that, they ultimately depend on us for their food.

Lonna and I have bird feeders in our yard, and birds are messy eaters. The sparrows, finches and chickadees like to scatter the seed all over as they eat. This abundance of food on the ground attracted roof rats, until my dogs and cats became interested in their comings and goings. Even when dogs and cats are well fed, they'll kill a prey animal—granted they'd rather play with it than eat it. Typically they'll chew on the unfortunate bird, rodent or lizard for a while then bring whatever's left to show you what big, bad hunters they are.

My Lab, Tucker, exhibited some weird behavior while Lonna and I were in Mexico on a vacation. Maisy, our Terrier, is good at escaping from what I thought was an escape-proof backyard and will dig under the fence or pull the childproof magnetic lock out and squeeze through the partially locked gate. Since she kept getting out,

Life is never dull with a house full of pets.

our dog sitter, Danielle, took her to board at our vet hospital. But the unexplained disappearance of his friend upset Tucker. He became a bundle of nerves and, for some reason, began compulsively eating all the birdseed on the ground. He even broke into and ate a new bag of birdseed. He ate so much birdseed that his poop looked like the seed sticks that you buy for pet birds. Life is never dull with a house full of pets.

When the ancestors of our domesticated dogs became comfortable sharing our living areas, begging for and stealing food naturally followed. Today some of our pets are very good at this scavenging and mooching behavior. My own pets do not wait out of sight or in the dark to get a handout; they take a more direct approach. Archie's begging tactic was the *non-blinking statue stare*—he'd watch our every eating movement without apparent eye movement. Sadie used the *"poor pitiful me, I'm starving" tactic* as if she had not eaten for days and might not last another hour. When more than one person is eating, the beggar uses the *tennis-match gaze*, constantly shifting his line of sight from one diner to the other. To enhance their begging tactics, some dogs will add pitiful shaking or soft whining.

If begging is not successful, more desperate measures are employed. As these come with the possibility of punishment, the thieves have to be quick. Dog rules: Any food left out on a counter or table within reach is fair game. If caught in the act, tremble and cower with guilt, and make it an Oscar-winning performance. My dogs are stars, but they're not alone.

One evening, Lonna and I were at our good friends Joe and Roni's house for dinner. We ventured outside for a moment to admire a brilliant, red sunset. When we went back in, I returned to the coffee table for more of the delicious crab dip in the hollowed-out bread bowl that I'd been enjoying moments before. When I did not find the appetizer, I asked Roni where she put it. As we searched the area we came across a contented, distended Dachshund named Schroeder who'd finished the bread bowl in five minutes and left not a crumb behind. I was worried about Schroeder becoming a patient after that feat, but he suffered only a mild stomachache the next day. I'm sure all of you have similar stories of a lovable furry thief.

So what's all this have to do with my Dog Dish Diet? It's about perspective. I think that sometimes we look at the strange and horrible things our dogs eat—rocks, twigs, disgusting dead things—and believe that a can or a cup of dog food has to be the healthiest option they've had all day. I grant you that commercial dog food is based on an *adequate* diet...albeit with a profit line that will keep shareholders happy. The problem is it's just not enough for the 30 to 40 percent of dogs that can't thrive on "merely adequate" and require different ingredients, a different type of food or supplemental fats and oils.

Create a Dog Dish Diet for Your Dog

Dog Food   People Food   Fats & Oils

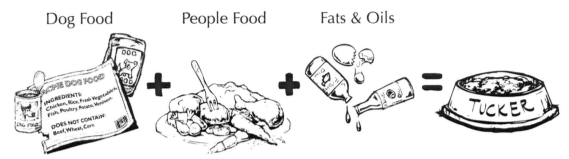

To prepare a Dog Dish Diet for your dog, you need to 1) consider the basic elements of good nutritional planning and 2) remember that your dog is an individual. What works for my Tucker may not be the best option for your dog. Start by choosing the **Type of Dog Food***: Kibble is convenient, but I prefer canned. Next select the* **Dog Food Ingredients** *with the right mix of proteins and carbs and that don't create an allergic reaction. Not all dogs have food allergies, but if you suspect a problem, start by cutting out the three most common allergens—beef, wheat and corn. For variety and good health, I supplement with healthful* **People Food***. Don't forget to add some good* **Fats and Oils***, including an egg yolk a couple times a week. Finally, be observant and adapt the Dog Dish Diet according to your dog's needs. I follow these rules when creating a Dog Dish Diet for Tucker and all my dogs.*

What's Wrong with Some Types of Commercial Food and Why

To understand how best to assess your dog's needs and put together the optimal feeding regimen, I think you need to know what's wrong with the modern, commercial dog diet. Welcome to Dog Food 101.

Cookie-cutter diet. The ideal dog food would contain all the ingredients needed to keep all dogs healthy and happy. The problem, of course, is that dogs, just like their owners, have different tolerances for different food ingredients and types of diets. Imagine that a *human* kibble company claims it has a complete-and-balanced people ration. If it contains peanuts, some people will go into anaphylactic shock, and a few will die. If the kibble is not gluten-free, people allergic to wheat will exhibit symptoms ranging from abdominal cramps and headaches to nausea, hives and swelling around the mouth.

I love seafood and shellfish, but if this so-called human kibble contains either, it could be perilous to others. A few shrimp can send a seafood-sensitive person to the hospital. Our diverse digestive and immune systems are based on genetics and life experience; they'll react differently to different ingredients.

The same conditions apply to our dogs. Slightly more than half of all dogs can eat any ingredient or type of food and not be plagued with weight, seizures, skin, ear, stomach or bowel problems. Another 30 percent to 40 percent need to eat diets that have non-allergenic ingredients to remain symptom-free. And all dogs will do best on a diet that is tailored to them...even my vegetarian patient. Suzie La Faille had two claims to fame: 1) She could unlock any cage door and escape, and 2) she is the only dog I've ever treated that *required* a vegetarian diet. She had a skin condition that only improved when her owner put her on a vegetarian diet.

As a result of my experiences, I counsel my clients to avoid beef, wheat and corn ingredients in the food, treats or table scraps they give their dogs. I advise them to find a dog food with chicken, turkey or duck as the protein and rice, potato and/or veggies as the carbohydrate. On occasion, a dog will need novel proteins and carbohydrates such as venison, fish, oats or barley, or even a vegetarian diet such as the one favored by Suzie La Faille. I'd considered all dogs to be meat eaters, but Suzie proved me wrong!

Remember, just because an advertisement, a friend, your favorite Uncle Ned or even your veterinarian recommends a certain food doesn't necessarily mean it's the best choice for *your* dog. Some dogs will need more or fewer calories, more healthful fats and oils, more moisture, different ingredients or fewer preservatives. And for all the advocating I do for chicken, I've known some dogs that were sensitive to chicken-and-rice diets but who tolerated beef- and wheat-based diets well. That's the opposite of the usual situation, and it shows why no one diet can be right for all dogs.

Several years ago Lori brought her dog Cleo into the office with symptoms of a urinary-tract infection. Cleo wanted outside to pee much more than usual, and it seemed to take a lot more effort to produce a very small amount of urine. To check for a urinary tract infection, I need a urine sample. Unfortunately, dogs will not voluntarily pee in a cup. The easiest way to get a urine sample in most dogs is to slide a small needle through the skin into the bladder and aspirate or suck the urine out with a syringe. Then we check the urine for red blood cells, white blood cells, bacteria, crystals and urine concentration. Cleo's urine had red blood cells, white blood cells and bacteria, a sure sign of a bladder infection. After Lori gave Cleo two weeks of antibiotics, she was cured. But two months later Cleo returned with the same symptoms; antibiotics again successfully took care of the infection. I warned Lori that some dogs are prone to bladder infections due to individual genetics, immunity and plumbing variations. During the next six months and several urinary-tract infections later, Lori correlated the bladder problems with pork. Every time the family ate pork chops and Cleo received a piece, she began exhibiting the same painful symptoms. This again reminded me that *any* food can be an allergen and cause a variety of health problems.

I realize this story may test my credibility with some of you, but consider this: Some food ingredients can boost immunity and general well-being, while other allergenic ingredients can cause inflammation and infections in the skin, stomach or bowel, and may affect other organs such as the liver, kidneys or bladder. If food allergies can cause inflammation in the ear canal, or be a factor in brain inflammation and promote seizures, there's no reason to think allergens couldn't inflame the bladder and promote bacterial infection. Take this as a useful lesson: If your dog exhibits any of the symptoms I am writing about here, you need to do your own tests and see if you can connect the problems to certain foods and treats in his diet.

Chews and Meaty-Wheaty Treats. When a young puppy is transported to our hospital for seizures often it has eaten a rawhide chew within the last 24 hours. Other dogs arrive on a daily basis with allergic reactions or pancreas and bowel problems after eating beef scraps or beef fat, rawhide-type chews or meaty-wheaty (beef/wheat) treats. The resulting allergic reaction and subsequent inflammation from consuming these types of ingredients can affect the skin, ears, stomach, bowel or brain and may initiate a cycle of chronic medical problems. I have no proof that seizures or other medical infirmities are caused by the meat by-products, beef, preservatives, wheat gluten or the chemicals used to treat the hide, but I do know that beef and wheat are the most common ingredients in treats, chews and dog foods. When these ingredients are avoided, many of my patients improve.

Your dog may not show any symptoms after eating rawhides or treats. Many dogs never suffer ill effects. However, some arrive at our hospital needing tests and extensive treatment for medical problems brought on by the canine junk food that owners lovingly feed as a treat. It's something to consider.

Kibble. Too much of anything is seldom a good thing. I used to think it was silly to buy canned food comprised of 70 percent water. Why

Ounce for ounce, canned dog food has about a third the calories of dry food.

would anyone pay good money for such a basic ingredient? Anyone could see that kibble was a better deal as it's 90 percent food and only 10 percent moisture. I've changed my mind. Water in the diet has real value. Vets and owners of some big breeds (e.g., Shepherds) know that bloat or gastric torsion can occur after eating a large meal of dry food. Heavy grain consumption causes a similar problem with the stomach of dairy cows. A high moisture content in food helps prevent the stomach from twisting and bloating, a dangerous condition in dogs. More water in food also dilutes the calories without leaving the animal feeling hungry. Here's the proof: A cup of dry food (8 ounces per volume but only about 4 ounces by weight) may contain almost 400 calories, or 80 to 100 calories per ounce by weight. On the other hand, a cup of canned food (8 ounces by weight and volume) averages about 280 calories or 35 calories per ounce. Ounce for ounce, dry food has about 40 percent more calories than canned dog food.

Most dogs "wolf" their kibbles with hardly a chew. The descriptive name of this manner of eating originated with the wolf's habit of eating large amounts of food at a time. Wolves have good reason to do this since there is no guarantee another wolf or predator won't come along and help itself to the remaining kill. Our domesticated pets, however, don't need to gorge. There will always be more food tomorrow although clearly some don't believe that. When dogs gorge on calorie-dense food, they take in a large amount of calories before the food even registers in the brain. As a result, many dogs become obese, eating more dry food or kibble than they require for either their nutrition or satisfaction. Even if your dog does not wolf its food, but is eating dry food and lots of treats (and is heavy) then I suspect the high-carbohydrate, calorie-dense dry food is to blame.

Some dogs simply cannot eat high-calorie food without packing on the weight.

Dry food (or kibble) is the most popular dog food on the market. It's very economical, easy to feed and convenient to store. Kibble is a mix of meat and grains that are pressure cooked, cooled and sprayed with flavor and fat to produce tasty, crunchy, bite-size biscuits. Best of all, you can scoop dry food right out of the bag and leave it in a bowl for days at a time.

Brands of kibble don't really differ substantively from one another. All contain approximately the same amounts and percentages of carbohydrates, proteins, fats and moisture. The low-moisture, high-carbohydrate formula makes kibble a very high-calorie diet. Kibble with chicken-and-rice, duck-and-potato or lamb-and-rice formulas may cause fewer food-related allergies than the beef, wheat and corn formulas, but does nothing to resolve the matter of low-moisture content and high-caloric intake.

I realize that millions of dogs eat dry food, biscuits and kibble every day and are in excellent health, but almost as many more canines are overweight, having seizures, and suffering from dry skin, allergies, itchy ears and stomach or bowel problems. They will enjoy a healthier life on a moister, lower-carbohydrate, hypo-allergenic diet.

Chapter Two

Your Dog May Be Telling You
It's Time for a Diet Change

*I*f you read through the list of the Top 10 reasons for a veterinary visit, you'd think that a veterinarian has it easy. After all, the most common reasons for a vet visit are ear and skin problems, stomach and bowel problems, painful joints, bladder infections and tumors. On the surface, these problems don't sound particularly challenging to diagnose or treat. Even your own experience would have you think that a wound or broken leg would be harder for a vet to deal with than a skin rash or inflamed ear.

The truth is that the wound and trauma cases require clear-cut treatments—cleaning the wound, taking an x-ray to check for internal injury, repairing a broken bone, and performing surgery when necessary. An itchy, painful, ear problem can be much more difficult to resolve permanently. Patient and owner are happy when the medication works and the symptoms go away. The problem is, all too often we are only treating symptoms because the source of the problem is not obvious. And no one's happy when the same problem comes back after the effect of the medication wears off. And the same is true for many skin ailments, upset stomachs and bowel problems.

Oliver's weight may be out of control, but perhaps I can sell my dog handle on eBay and make some money!

I can tell you for a fact that fully one third of the visits to our hospital involve a Top 10 condition that can become chronic (meaning that the same symptoms come back several times after treatment). These chronic medical problems leave your dog miserable, you spending more money and your vet feeling helpless and frustrated.

Canine Obesity: A Serious Epidemic

The most common health problem I see in our hospital is not even listed among the Top 10 ailments. Its omission, however, doesn't make

 Top 10 Dog Ailments

Veterinary Pet Insurance Top 10 Claims by Incident in Dogs (2008)

1. Ear Infections
2. Skin Allergies
3. Pyoderma (hotspots/bacterial skin infections)
4. Gastritis/Vomiting (stomach upsets)
5. Enteritis/Diarrhea
6. Urinary Tract Infections
7. Benign Skin Tumors
8. Osteoarthritis
9. Eye Inflammation
10. Hypothyroidism

The surprising results of changing the diets of my own dogs made me wonder if any of these other Top 10 aliments might have similar nutritional causes. Could the constant parade of shaking, itching dogs scooting through our hospital with dry, flaky, inflamed skin; red, painful, gooey ears; stomach upsets; and diarrhea be affected by allergens in the diet, the type of diet, or the mix of nutrients in the diet—instead of by fleas and pollen as I'd been taught? In veterinary school, I'd learned that skin, ear, stomach, and bowel problems were only infrequently a result of food allergies or intolerances. My positive experience with nutritional counseling leads me to believe that at least six of the symptoms on the Top 10 list may have a common, nutritional denominator.

I have found that a healthier diet may actually prevent, decrease and often cure many of the common chronic problems listed in the Top 10.

canine obesity any less serious. The most disturbing irony is that I'm often presented with dogs that seem to get heavier and heavier, even when their owners try to restrict the amount of food they eat. A young Yorkie I saw recently is starting to resemble a ball. "He's getting so fat, he's hard to pick up," his owner jokingly explained. "Soon I may need to fashion a handle and sling for him!" We need to stop and ask ourselves: Why is there an epidemic of overweight dogs? Why is there a weight-loss pill being marketed for dogs? Here's what I've learned.

Many dogs that eat dry food are weight challenged because they eat too much, too fast. Many dogs practically inhale two or more cups of dry food in minutes. The amount they eat is often more than they need. A cup of dry food, like other dry, high-carbohydrate, low-moisture foods, is packed with calories and only 10 percent water. In other words, each 8-ounce cup of dry food contains 0.8 ounces or about 1 teaspoon of water—that is, if the water hasn't evaporated

> *Why is there an epidemic of overweight dogs? Why is there a weight-loss pill being marketed for dogs?*

after the bag's been sitting open in your pantry for a few weeks. That leaves a lot of calorie-laden ounces in one cup of dry food.

You're wondering why the amount of water contained in dog food should make such a difference. The answer lies with the natural wolf diet and other natural foods, including fruit, vegetables and meats. These all have higher water and lower carbohydrate contents than kibble, which may be the key to a healthful formula. Canned food; raw food; healthful, human food; and homemade concoctions all put more moisture and fewer carbohydrates per serving into our dogs' diets.

A cup of kibble or dry dog food contains 8 ounces of kibble by volume and 4 ounces by weight due to the irregular shapes of the kibble and air spaces. Each cup of kibble would contain 10 percent water and 70 percent carbohydrates. That would be 5.6 ounces of carbs by volume (measuring cup) and 2.8 ounces by weight (scale). The weight and volume of a cup of canned food are almost the same because there are no air spaces as with the kibble. Canned food is 75 percent water or 6 ounces; the carbs are just 35 percent of the remaining 2 ounces (or 0.8 ounces). When we compare the two, we see clearly that 2.8

ounces of carbs by weight in dry food versus 0.8 ounces of carbs in canned food means that you'll be giving your dog 3.5 times more carbohydrates per serving when you feed him dry food.

So what's the bottom line? Being very dry, and having two to three times the carbohydrates by weight, means dry food or kibble contains 40 percent more calories than the same amount of canned food. Kibble may have crunch, but canned food's high water content naturally dilutes the carbohydrate and calorie count. By choosing canned food, you'll be giving your dog fewer carbohydrates per cup and, thus, fewer calories per serving. This may explain why many pooches that eat kibble are, unfortunately, super-sized. Our good friends Marty and Val Marinovich adopted a Pug named Chino that became quite heavy eating kibble. To reduce the calories, Val added green beans to half the amount of kibble. Chino lost enough weight to finally fit through the doggie door.

Many dogs eating dry food are able to eat the right amount to maintain their weight or burn off those extra calories, just as some people are able

It's the Real Numbers that May be Making Rover Fat

To prevent overfeeding and obesity when giving a dog dry food or kibble, you need a rough idea of the calories contained in an ounce. Simply, you need to know how much to feed your dog. This can be a bit confusing, so hang with me. Because of its shape (and the fact that air is injected into the kibble during processing), one cup of kibble does not really contain 8 ounces of food. The air spaces around and in the kibble take up space, so one cup of kibble contains less than one cup of food ingredients.

To get the picture, visualize those nasty, peanut-shaped foam pieces that escape from boxes containing your mail-order treasures. If you filled a measuring cup with foam peanuts to the 8-ounce line (no easy task) and then took them out and crushed them to remove all the air, the compacted foam peanut material might only reach the 2-ounce line. The same thing is true with kibble. So how many ounces of food are in a level cup of kibble? On average, about 3 ounces or 4 ounces of food; the rest is air. Remember this image if you need to visualize or figure out the difference between weight of food and its volume.

to eat anything and stay trim (we're jealous of them!), while others gain weight on a small amount of food. If your dog enjoys eating and is not very active, it will become weight challenged on most commercial, dry-food diets.

> *By choosing canned food, you'll be giving your dog fewer carbohydrates per cup and, thus, fewer calories per serving. This may explain why many pooches that eat kibble are, unfortunately, super-sized.*

If your dog is just a touch overweight, substituting healthful, low-calorie human food (such as baby carrots, green beans, deli meat or a small piece of chicken) for high-calorie biscuits and treats—**along with reducing the amount of dry food**—will help. More exercise will also burn those extra calories and is good for the heart, muscles and joints, as well as for the dog owner. More exercise could mean a daily walk, playing fetch or catch, a romp at the dog park or maybe a new doggie playmate.

Obesity in dogs can lead to arthritis and joint pain, making it harder to enjoy life. The more pounds per square inch of force applied to a dog's joints or spine, the more likely it will suffer from back problems, hip problems or other joint problems. Picture a dog's back as a bridge and its legs as pillars. The extra weight deforms the vertebrae and discs of the bridge as gravity pulls them downward. The constant pull and torque of extra weight overloads the structure and may lead to vertebrae and disc damage known as bulging discs, collapsing discs, spinal arthritis and joint problems from extra weight damaging the cartilage and ligaments of the joint. As the damage sets in, dogs find it increasingly difficult or impossible to jump on or off the couch or bed and into or out of the car. Eventually they will be stressed simply trying to make it up and down the stairs. Avoiding these problems by helping your dog lose weight may not require special medical diets or a weight-loss pill. When you know more about ingredients and different types of diets, you can make healthful choices for your weight-challenged one.

I want to come back as a dog in the next life. At this moment, I see Tucker, my Yellow Lab, lying on his back on *his* leather couch with his legs straight up in the air...snoring. Most of the time when we are gone during the day, or inactive ourselves, our dogs are inactive. Their enviable lifestyle only requires enough calories to keep body systems running. But an epidemic of full-figured pooches proves that there are more calories in their diets than dogs need.

 Quick Fix When Feeding Spot Dry Dog Food

If your dog seems to do pretty well on dry food, but you want to help him lose a few extra pounds, here are some quick, simple fixes:

- Reduce the portion size of the food your dog is eating,

- Change the brand of food to one with fewer calories per serving,

- Soak half the normal portion of dry food in water or chicken broth (or you could use turkey, fish or lamb broth left over from your cooking) to make up your dog's normal amount of food with half the calories. Soaking the kibble dilutes the calories, while your dog gets the same volume of food and feels full and happy. In a few minutes, these dry kibbles will soak up the liquid and look like a normal portion, but contain fewer calories.

- Cut usual food serving in half and supplement with canned green beans.

- Replace 1 cup of kibble with 1 cup of canned food.

Beware the Chewy Treat

Rawhide chews, chewy treats, and biscuits and dog snacks with wheat and beef ingredients appear to have a big role in causing gastrointestinal problems in our pets. When I began my nutritional counseling, I made sure my clients knew about the different types of foods and ingredients in their dog's diet. However, after a short time I realized I'd been neglecting to counsel them about feeding treats. When I asked what their dogs ate, many clients would not mention treats. Or they'd insist, "Treats are good for their teeth!" In my opinion, most treats have very little effect on tartar, but they are good for my bottom line, leading to at least two client visits per day.

Canine Skin Issues: Why Sweet-em's Skin Itches

After obesity, the second most common problem I encounter relates to the health of the skin. This is pretty universally true among vets and why skin and ear problems are the top two ailments on the Veterinary Pet Insurance list.

Perhaps you recognize some set of these symptoms in your own dog: dry, flaky skin; red, itchy skin; oily, yeasty skin; or bacterial skin infections. These conditions, along with red, goopy ears, make up at least one-third of my daily appointments. These painful and often ugly conditions can make life miserable for pet and owner. Antibiotics, antihistamines, antifungal medications, medicated baths, cortisone injections, pills and ear medications may help to relieve the pain and inflammation of these conditions temporarily. But as I've seen all too often, if a dog's underlying allergies and nutritional needs are not addressed, the itching, inflammation and pain will return. Allergenic ingredients and a lack of the necessary amounts and types of fats and oils in most commercial diets may be leading to unhealthy skin in your dog.

Abnormal Puking and Pooping: Symptoms Not to Take Lightly

The third most common problem requiring vet visits involves abnormal puking and pooping. These conditions, along with being squeamish at the sight of blood, are probably the two biggest reasons why most people decide not to become veterinarians. Nausea, vomiting and diarrhea can be caused by food allergies, but life-threatening conditions such as parvovirus, pancreatitis, parasites, internal organ problems and infections can also cause these symptoms. *So it's important you get to root of the problem.*

Food allergies are usually characterized by milder, chronic symptoms that plague the owner with frequent piles of vomit in the house. Many young dogs and some older dogs will eat plastic, wood or some utterly disgusting thing and then get very nauseous and vomit for a day or two. Tucker once ate pieces of my truck seat. If a dog vomits several times in a short period, or looks very ill, it is definitely time for a vet visit. It's always better to err on the side of caution if you observe a lot of vomiting and diarrhea. Something might be stuck somewhere in the stomach or intestine, or the dog may have an infection. On the other hand, if a dog vomits a few times but is otherwise

> *...if a dog vomits a few times but is otherwise frisky and happy, you can often give him half of a Pepcid tablet and wait 24 hours to see if the vomiting stops. This is a general rule of thumb, however, not a diagnosis.*

frisky and happy, you can often give him half of a Pepcid tablet and wait 24 hours to see if the vomiting stops. (Note: Only use this treatment for one or two days without a diagnosis.)

Is Your Dog Suffering from Allergies?

Allergy symptoms are easy to diagnose but often hard to treat. For example, people affected with allergies are miserable at certain times of the year when the pollen count is high. Doctors can help their itchy eyes, runny noses and painful sinus problems with antihistamines, antibiotics or cortisones, but the symptoms will return with a vengeance given time and more pollen. That is the normal course with allergic conditions. The symptoms wax and wane depending on pollen count and allergen exposures.

Allergens, however, are not species specific. Veterinarians may spend up to 30 percent of their day treating dogs with inflammation from allergic reactions. Fleabites, various plant and tree pollens, molds, contact with grasses and weeds, and certain food ingredients can bring about allergic reactions. Each of these allergens may cause symptoms that make our pets uncomfortable.

The most common signs of allergies in dogs are inflamed, itchy skin and/or ears; red, oozy, crusty sores called hotspots; recurring upset stomach and bowel problems; and even seizures. Classic symptoms may be: Dogs susceptible to pollens and molds, for example, might continually lick and chew at their paws when the pollen count is very high. If the flea population rises, flea allergy or sensitivity to fleas often causes dogs to chew right where their butt joins their tail. They work at a spot often quite noisily.

Almost all these symptoms can have an underlying allergic cause that makes it harder to permanently "cure" them...until now. Once the medial diagnosis rules out other causes and suggests an allergic reaction, I first recommend medication to relieve the immediate symptoms and give the dog relief. Second, I advise positive changes to the diet. In my experience, food allergies can cause any number of symptoms—from hotspots and bad ears to hives and seizures—that mimic those from fleas, pollen and even epilepsy. It comes down to dogs eating ingredients in their diet to which they're allergic. If something as easy as a better diet can make such a big difference with so many different canine issues, doesn't it make sense to give it a try?

How Allergies Develop: The Immune System Fights Back

The immune system works 24/7 protecting against viral, bacterial and parasitic invaders from the air, the environment and food. White blood cells, such as lymphocytes, roam the nooks and crannies of blood and lymph systems like police watching out for troublemakers. Let's use this *Law and Order* analogy to understand what happens: When a white blood cell finds a perpetrator, it apprehends, fingerprints and disables it and then calls for reinforcements. The "fingerprint" is used to manufacture antibodies in case there are a large number of perpetrators. Antibodies manufactured from this fingerprint circulate throughout the body looking for more "perps" to disable.

Most of the time the immune system works efficiently and effectively, keeping invaders from entering delicate areas and causing problems. But occasionally wires get crossed, and pollen or food proteins are mistaken for invaders and troublemakers. The immune system attacks these pollens or digested food particles as if they are dangerous. Due to the high numbers of pollen or food particles in the system, the body calls in reinforcements (cells and antibodies) to join the fight and disable what are actually harmless proteins. Once this happens, the immune system identifies these protein particles as foreign and dangerous and will react with a vengeance every time they're encountered. That is how food or other normal, day-to-day pollens cause allergic reactions. The body *mistakes* normal food or pollen proteins for dangerous invaders and reacts accordingly. These reactions cause the symptoms that make our pets (and us) miserable.

Help with Allergies: The Challenge of Tests and Medications

When vets want to solve a problem, they need to gather as much information as possible to rule out any underlying bad conditions. Treating an infection with antibiotics or inflamed skin with cortisone or antihistamines, for example, will not be successful if the condition is complicated by cancer, diabetes, parasites or other organ problems. To rule out these types of complications, we first do blood, fecal, urine and skin tests to check the blood cells, electrolytes, thyroid gland, liver, kidneys, blood sugar, pancreas, adrenal glands, intestines and muscles. We also do a careful check of the largest organ of all—the skin—for infections or parasites.

Thanks to television, the common belief is that we put the dog's blood into our blood-analysis machine and within a few minutes, a piece of paper comes out with the answer on it, the machine having automatically checked for medical problems, cancer or poisons. That would certainly simplify my job. In reality, blood tests have to be interpreted. We must consider the age of our patient along with what we see, feel and hear in the exam room as well as any other medical conditions that must be taken into consideration when interpreting results.

Blood tests measure the stuff that a gland or organ puts in or takes out of the blood. When an organ is old, infected or disturbed by a tumor, it may not be able to remove toxic matter from the blood as efficiently, or it may leak "organ juice" into the blood system. Glands (thyroid, adrenal and pancreas) can produce too much or too little glandular "juice." By knowing each gland's or organs standard enzyme or product level, we're able to determine if they are healthy.

The hard part is figuring out if age, genetics, infection, tumors, toxins or another malfunctioning organ or gland are affecting the organ or gland in question. It doesn't sound quite as straightforward as it does on TV medical shows, does it? Most of the time blood tests and other lab results are clear. But sometimes the results don't match with what we see. One dog can register abnormal levels on some tests of a blood panel and yet appear happy and healthy with no obvious symptoms. Another dog can have normal blood values and be in critical condition.

To make matters more difficult, several common problems we diagnose using laboratory testing actually mimic the symptoms with an allergic or nutritional basis. This is where our challenge really gets interesting. Take, for example, *hypothyroidism* or low levels of thyroid hormone in the bloodstream, which can make the body sluggish. Labs and Goldens are the most common victims, with the usual symptoms being weight gain and lack of energy. Low thyroid pooches are also prone to skin infections and parasites because their skin and immune system are not working efficiently. Instead of a good hair coat, low thyroid levels result in a very poor hair coat with hair color lighter than normal. If the test for thyroid shows a low level, thyroid medication is given orally for life to raise the thyroid levels and body processes to normal. When a dog gains weight while consuming the recommended amount of food, testing for thyroid function can help determine if the weight gain is due to food or to a low amount of circulating thyroxin and the resulting lower metabolism.

Likewise autoimmune diseases can mimic allergies and parasites. These tricky conditions are hard to diagnose. Blood testing and skin biopsies are sometimes needed. These situations occur when the immune system attacks the body and the skin—in essence, one becomes allergic to oneself.

Collectively these situations make veterinarians only wish their blood-analysis machines offered diagnoses on a printout. My dream machine would say: *liver problem because of an* Escherichia coli *infection*. And I'd say, "Ah ha! I thought so."

Fleas, Pollens, Molds and Foods...Oh My

Allergies in dogs are caused by three common allergen groups:

- Fleas
- Pollens, grasses and molds
- Allergenic food ingredients (most often wheat, beef and corn)

Depending on the flea count, what pollen is in the air, what is growing on the ground, what a dog has rubbed against or what treats have been consumed, we can see a parade of inflamed canines head-shaking and butt-scratching their way through our hospital.

The Pesky Flea. Flea allergy is the most common allergy in dogs. You can check for these pesky creatures by parting the hair and looking on the skin near the tail, neck or belly. Fleas are small, dark, thin objects moving through the hair, and the tiny specks that you think are dirt are often flea poop. If you want to gross out your family, comb the tiny black specks onto a paper towel and moisten them. If they are flea poop, the specks will turn into red splotches because flea poop is largely composed of your dog's blood. A flea's life consists of sucking blood, pooping it out and birthing more fleas. If the specks stay black, they really are dirt.

Fortunately fleas are easy to treat with monthly topical drops (e.g., Advantage) that usually reduce their numbers quickly. Continued monthly applications will keep those numbers down. All animals that have had contact with the flea-infested one also need to be treated. Other pets can have fleas but may not suffer as much itching because they're not as sensitive or allergic to the bites. Remember to treat cats that roam outside your yard and bring more fleas back home to your dog.

Fleas fall into the larger category of *parasites*—a whole host of creatures, many of which are microscopic, crawling on or in the skin, living in the hair follicles or growing on the hair shaft. The body reacts to these as invaders, and indeed they are. The skin becomes inflamed and infected, and the hair coat is terrible. Like fleas, most common parasites, such as mites and ringworm, are diagnosed by seeing them, scraping the skin, or plucking a hair and looking for them on a microscope slide. While they can be treated, not all cases resolve easily. But fleas and all parasites need to be ruled out when looking for the source of Scratchy's inflamed and itchy skin and poor coat.

Pollens, Grasses and Mold. The second most common group of allergens in dogs is the same one that causes hay fever in humans. Allergies to pollens, molds, grasses, dust mites and household fibers can cause two different types of inflammation, depending on how they are contracted. The first syndrome—defined in medical terminology as *Atopy*—will cause sneezing, runny eyes, painful red ears, paw chewing and general itching and discomfort whenever pollens, molds and grasses come into contact with the membranes of the eyes, nose, sinuses and lungs during normal activity and breathing. Atopy itching can lead to loss of hair and skin infections, which, in turn, cause more itching, licking, biting and, often, pain.

> **Flea Test:** Comb your pet's hair and catch any dark specks onto a paper towel and moisten them. If it's flea poop, the specks will turn red because it's largely composed of your dog's blood. If the specks stay black, they are dirt.

The second syndrome involves inflammation from grasses and pollens infiltrating the places where the skin comes in direct contact with allergens. Dogs usually experience inflammation from contact allergies on their feet and other hairless areas. Pollens and molds are impossible to avoid, especially if you are a dog and your nose, eyes and body are so close to the ground.

Complicating infections plague allergy sufferers. As anyone with frequent hay fever and congested sinuses knows, bacteria love inflamed sinuses. Inflamed sinuses are warm and filled with thick juice. First the sinuses become inflamed; then bacteria are able to gain a foothold and grow. Until the bacteria are cleared, the allergic symptoms persist. The same types of conditions exist in the inflamed skin and ears of dogs. The skin and ears become excessively oily, waxy or gooey and then are over-run by bacteria and yeast. Until these "claim jumper" infections are cleared, the allergy victim will continue to be miserable. We diagnose staph and yeast infections by

Fifty percent of all dogs have dry skin that is easily treated, in most cases, with the addition of extra oils and fats to the diet.

swabbing the skin or ears and looking under the microscope to find the pesky critters. Antibiotic and antifungal pills, lotions, and shampoos help rid the body of both the inflammation and the bacteria and yeast infections that take up residence in the inflamed skin.

Allergy testing usually tells us which pollens, molds or grasses trigger sensitive reactions in the dog. Higher scores for any particular pollen, mold or grass can mean it's a troublemaker. We then administer shots containing the higher-scoring, troublesome allergens in the hope that over a long period of time the immune system gets used to the injected allergens and may not react as much next time it encounters them. In my experience, these injections may reduce the unpleasant symptoms in about one third of the Atopic dogs we treat.

Cortisone and cyclosporine can also be used to suppress the immune response and allergic reactions to the troublesome allergens. Cortisones such as dexamethasone and prednisone are great for acute inflamed, itchy, painful conditions, but both can cause side effects with long-term use.

Who's The Most Itchy of All?

Selective breeding has produced some dogs with a higher incidence of allergies than other dog breeds and mixes. Labradors, Golden Retrievers, Boxers, Bulldogs, Mastiffs, Char Peis, Poodles, German Shepherds, Jack Russell Terriers, Rottweilers, Pit Bulls, West Highland Terriers and Cocker Spaniels tend to have allergy issues. Terriers suffer from an allergy to pollens more than other breeds. And nearly every day a Lab or two come into our practice to be examined and treated for ear inflammation. The Labrador breed is definitely over-represented in the ear category. Some dogs have more sensitivity to flea bites, others develop painful feet from running on the grass and still more can be unable to tolerate food ingredients such as wheat gluten, corn and beef. Regardless the cause, the resulting symptoms of skin, ear, stomach and bowel problems make them all equally miserable.

It may sound funny for a vet to say, but I hate to sentence any dog with mild to moderate symptoms to long-term medication unless it is absolutely necessary to help with discomfort, pain, medical syndromes or seizures. I find it more rewarding to treat my pets and patients both nutritionally AND medically to address the multiple causes of many common problems involving the skin, ears, stomach and bowels. When I address nutritional issues and make changes to the *type* of food fed, the *ingredients* of the food and treats and the *amount* of healthful fats and oils in the diet, I find that many dogs improve and I'm able to reduce or eliminate the need for long-term medication and constant treatment.

That said, I realize that I'll always have a few situations that require the prescription of a long-term course of medications.

After Years of Ears...

Dogs plagued with red, inflamed, itchy, painful and gooey ears may represent 10 percent to 30 percent of appointments in a veterinary hospital on any given day. After so many years and ears, it's disconcerting to walk into the exam room after hearing my assistant say, "It's a dog with ear problems." I know what's coming next: "Doc, my dog has been shaking his head and digging at his ears. He was rubbing his ears outside on the ground, and I think something is down in there. I have used the ear medicine from the pet store, and it did not help. Could it be mites?"

"Dogs rarely get mites," I reply, "but in the spring, summer and fall, big fat ear ticks like to live down in the ear canal." Looking up, I see my client visualizing this catastrophe in utter horror. Then I continue: "Other causes of painful ears can be plant awns—sharp, long processes of grass-seed casings—such as the foxtail that find their way into the canal. Swimming, floppy ears, small ear canals and hairy ear canals that restrict air movement, increase humidity and impede the normal flow of wax out of the ear...all of these are potential sources of irritation."

A glance at the medical records often shows regular attendance at our hospital, so I add, "Because your dog has been having the same problems for a while and the records show that antibiotics, anti-inflammatories, ear medications and treatment seem to offer only temporary relief, your dog's ear problems may be caused by allergies to pollens, molds, grasses or certain food ingredients." The response is usually, "So does he get a shot, some pills, and some ear medication? Could I get something different? The last medication you gave us did not work."

Here are the facts: If the pain and irritation are caused by ticks, plant awns (foxtails) or an excess of hair and wax, removal of the offending objects and medicating the ears will usually solve the problem. Swimming dogs may need medication or cleaning after they swim.

Dogs with ear problems caused by pollens, molds, grasses or food ingredients such as wheat, beef and corn are not as easy to treat. When the pollen count is high or when they eat an ingredient to which they're sensitive, their ears turn red and start to itch. The irritated glands of the ear canal flood the canal with a gooey wax that, in a few days, can become a yeasty, toxic, bacterial soup.

The excess wax, inflammation and infections can be treated with ear cleaners, anti-inflammatories and antibiotics, but if the cause of the inflammation is ignored, infection will reoccur. I've treated thousands of ears and have seen better results using nutrition and medical treatments simultaneously. Today, my patients with ear problems leave with the typical ear medications and ear washes along with information on feeding healthful food ingredients; avoiding allergens in dog food, treats, chews and snacks; and adding healthful fats and oils. Taken together, these steps can help the red-eared, painful one avoid future ear episodes.

I have not kept track of the exact numbers or percentages of dogs with ear problems that improve when fed differently, but I do know that among the 1000s of clients, the majority report positive results when nutritional and medical treatments are used side-by-side. In my mind, the fact that so many ear problems improve when known allergens are avoided is further evidence that allergies to food ingredients are responsible for a significant number of skin and ear conditions. *Want to know the best thing? It's easy to treat allergy symptoms with nutritional therapy. You don't need to buy special supplements. You just need to monitor ingredients, and add wholesome ones. That is my Dog Dish Diet in a nutshell.*

Food Allergies. The third, and last, group of allergens is the one dogs encounter in their food. I alluded to this in the last section, but it's significant enough to warrant a separate discussion. In veterinary school I was taught that allergies to food ingredients cause the fewest symptoms. But after almost 30 years of practice, I believe that while food allergies may not be as dramatic, or as easy, to diagnose, they're every bit as prevalent as flea allergies, canine hay fever and contact allergies.

 Will a Hypoallergenic Diet Make a Difference?

A diet is called hypoallergenic when the ingredients are those known to cause the fewest allergic symptoms. Common hypoallergenic diets usually contain protein sources, such as chicken, duck, turkey and lamb, or novel protein sources such as fish, venison and bison. This last group of ingredients is termed "novel" because most dogs will not have had the opportunity to eat venison, fish or bison and develop allergies to them. Diets with these novel ingredients are more costly and are used when dogs continue to suffer and show symptoms even when fed the more common hypoallergenic diets.

When you feed food ingredients that do not cause inflammation and allergies, most irritating symptoms will slowly decrease and may disappear completely in weeks or months. Chronic ear and skin problems, even persistent nausea and diarrhea often need less medication and, in time, may not need any medication at all. Because we are repairing a complex biological system, the positive effects of nutritional changes often take a little longer to manifest than if we'd simply administered a pill or a shot. But a happier, healthier pet is often the long-term result...and well worth it.

Medication Advice

Your dog can be tricked into taking an over-the-counter antihistamine pill such as Benadryl or Claritin by hiding it in cheese, a chunk of chicken or turkey hotdog. Hydrocortisone cream can be rubbed into the red, itchy skin, ear or butt for temporary relief until you can take your pooch to the veterinarian. If your dog is a chronic sufferer, it's a good idea to save a few pills from the last visit for the next event. It could save you from an expensive emergency visit, and make Slurpy comfortable enough to sleep through the night. Only use medication for a few days without consulting your vet.

As I've explained, dogs and humans are allergic to some foods because sometimes a pollen or food protein will trick the immune system into thinking it is an invading virus, bacteria or toxin. The antibodies and cellular armies of the body battle the food molecule or chemical as though it is a dangerous enemy. When I tell owners with allergy-prone dogs to watch for allergenic ingredients such as beef, wheat and corn in the diet, some reply, "I thought beef was good for dogs." *Here's the truth:*

> *In the many years I've been practicing, I've treated 1000s of dogs that have had allergic reactions to beef, wheat and/or corn.*

In the many years I've been practicing, I've treated 1000s of dogs that have had allergic reactions to beef, wheat and/or corn. Either the ancestors of the dog did not have bovine and grain on the menu, or we've altered the meat and grain enough through breeding and/or processing that some dogs just can't tolerate them. For those of you that feed raw beef or diets with beef ingredients, and your dogs are fine, remember that I am *not* making blanket claims about evil protein sources. Rather, I'm reporting my experiences. My data are what I've seen firsthand, and I've seen enough problems associated with beef, wheat and corn diets to feel compelled to bring this to your attention.

When beef, wheat and corn ingredients are in a dog's food or treats, or fed as scraps, allergic dogs will itch, rub their ears, scoot, vomit, eat grass, get the runs or lie about looking miserable. Some of you lucky folks own dogs that get gassy after eating beef. Eliminating wheat, beef and corn makes many dogs feel better. This means that if your dog is allergic, then wheat gluten, beef, beef by-products, beef liver (sometimes just labeled liver), meat digest and meat by-products should NOT be on the list of ingredients of the food or treats you are feeding your dog. *If your dog is allergic to beef, the most popular hypoallergenic choices for meats or proteins are chicken, duck and lamb.*

Wheat and corn are the grains that cause the most allergy symptoms in dogs. Since it's hard to know which allergen is affecting your droopy one the most, I usually recommend avoiding both. *I've found that rice, potato and vegetables are the carbohydrates that cause the fewest allergy symptoms.*

Diet and Allergies: The Itch Bag Explained

Pretend that your dog's body is an allergen bag—a container filled by different allergens throughout the day. Some allergens are sucked in from the air; some are rubbed on the skin or injected through it via fleas, ticks and mosquitoes; and others are eaten. Now picture an itch line on the allergen bag. This line represents the number of allergens your dog needs to inhale, rub on, get injected with or eat before he starts to itch. If the allergen load does not reach the itch line, your dog's skin will not itch, turn red or break out in hives. But when different allergens such as fleas, pollens, molds and food ingredients fill up the bag past the itch line, your dog will itch or have other common allergy symptoms.

Every day the itch bag starts filling again as Scratchy comes in contact with fleas, pollens and mold spores or consumes the ingredients in a meaty-wheaty meal or treat. The bag will fill slowly or

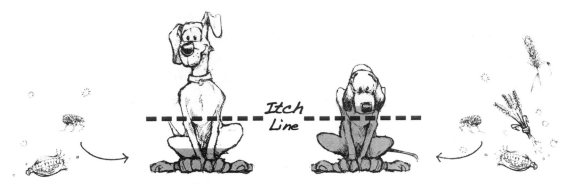

Pretend your dog's body is an allergen bag...

quickly, depending on what the itchy one is allergic to and the number of allergens in the environment or food. It's a cumulative effect so anything we can do to reduce the allergen contact in a normal day will help decrease Scratchy's chance of reaching the itch line and therefore help keep him comfortable.

Using antihistamines or anti-inflammatories such as Claritin, Benadryl or cortisone raise the itch line for anywhere from a few hours to a few days, but if the cause is not addressed, the symptoms *will* return. Although I find this visualization a plausible explanation, I admit it's my own concept with no research to back it up, but it makes just as much sense to me as other explanations.

Just as people can be allergic to several different allergens at the same time so too can our dogs. The big difference is that the only allergens we can control in our pets' lives are those in the food and those caused by fleas, which is why nutrition is so important. Feeding a hypoallergenic diet gives the skin, ears, stomach and bowel fewer allergens with which to react. The fewer allergens consumed, the less chance your dog will suffer from the symptoms of allergies.

As long as we're talking about my theories, I'll throw in another one. I believe that adding essential fats and oils makes the skin healthier and less reactive to allergens. Picture the doggie itch bag with its own personal itch line again. When the skin is healthier from adding polyunsaturated and monounsaturated fatty acids in the diet (e.g., fish, olive or canola oils or eggs), and thus is not as dry or prone to itching, it might take more allergens to cause inflammation.

In short, we're accomplishing two things with a better diet: First, we're reducing the number of allergens to slow the filling of the itch bag. And second, by adding essential fats and oils, we are making the skin healthier and less prone to dryness and inflammation. This goes for people too: Those of you who tend toward dry or inflamed skin know how miserable the symptoms can be. Adding good fats and oils to the diet may make your skin healthier and move your itch line higher...for as long as you continue to include the healthful oils in your diet. It's the same with our dogs: The allergens they come in contact with fill the bag to the same level, but healthier skin is less reactive, the daily volume of allergens may no longer reach the raised itch line, and Scratchy feels better.

Depending on the flea count, what pollen is in the air, what is growing on the ground, what the dog has rubbed against or what treats have been consumed, we can see a parade of inflamed canines head-shaking and butt-scratching their way through our hospital. It's frustrating to spend so much of my day treating conditions that I know will come back after the effects of medication wear off. That said, and after treating thousands of dogs with skin, ear, stomach and bowel problems and after experiencing more lasting success when I treated them both medically and nutritionally, it's obvious to me that almost all dogs benefit from healthful changes to their diet, regardless of what allergens bother them the most.

Chapter Three

Identifying the
Most Nutritional Options

By now, you are probably beginning to see that the health of your dog is a complex thing and that treatment often requires more than a pill or a shot for resolution. Yes, medication can give quick relief of allergy symptoms, but it may take a change of diet to get to the root of a problem. Remember, when it comes to dog diets, there is no one-size-fits-all solution. The diet changes you eventually make will be the result of your observation, evaluation, common sense and maybe even a little trial and error. Let's explore some of those options.

The Case for Omega Oils and Essential Fatty Acids

In 1930, Burr, Burr and Miller from the University of Minnesota published a study demonstrating that fat is an essential nutrient in the diet of rats. They removed all the fats and oils from the diet of weanling rats, and then added different types of fats or oils to each experimental group to see which fats or oils had the most positive effects on growth rate and health. They found that linoleic acid (what would later be identified as essential fatty acids) offered considerable benefit. Today we know these substances as Omega 3 and Omega 6.

At the time, Omega 3 and Omega 6 were called "essential fatty acids" because the body cannot manufacture them AND they need to be present in the diet to maintain optimum health. Without them, the rats had poor growth rates; dry, inflamed skin; and a poor hair coat. The groups with omega fatty acids added back to otherwise fat-free diets showed the best growth and health. You've no doubt heard the names of these critical fats and oils in advertisements and have seen them on labels and signs in the supermarket and pharmacy. Numerous nutritional articles have touted their importance to the skin, heart, reproductive and mental health of humans and other mammals...including our dogs.

Our diets consist of percentages of protein, carbohydrate and fat ingredients, the correct proportions of which are a subject of measurement and constant debate among nutritionists. Even though most animals in the wild and most people, for that matter, thrive on more fat in their diets, veterinary nutritionists and commercial, dog food companies have decided that all dogs do just fine on diets with 10 percent to 15 percent fat. *I feel this is a serious mistake.*

You should do the research and weight the risks and benefits of Salmonella or E. coli infection, but personally I mix a raw egg yolk in my dog's food two or three times a week.

My introduction to the importance of the right fats came several years ago when a client brought in a bottle of "skin wonder medication" that she bought from a local pet store. "You really ought to

> *Even though most animals in the wild and most people, for that matter, thrive on more fat in their diets, veterinary nutritionists and commercial dog food companies have decided that dogs do just fine on diets with 10 percent to 15 percent fat.*

sell this product," she said. "It cleared up my dog's skin after I ran out of all the expensive medication you gave me that didn't work." I glanced at the bottle's ingredients and noted B vitamins, yeast extract and fish oil. "Thanks for showing me," I said as I conjured up visions of dubious snake-oil remedies and the traveling potions salesman in *The Wizard of Oz*. Years later, I now know what I should have been seeing.

For supple skin and a sleek hair coat, some dogs require more good fats and essential fatty acids than are present in the average commercial diet. The main ingredients in many oral supplements are the omega oils. So one of the first things I recommend to clients when their dog has skin and ear problems is to supplement the diet with the omega fatty acids and monounsaturated acids contained in oils such as fish oil, olive oil, canola oil and egg yolks. If the commercial dog food contained enough of these fats and oils already, the addition of fats and oils to the diet would make no difference. In my experience, however, it almost always does.

Fish-oil capsules have become a morning treat at the Martinez house. The dogs hear the rattle when I grab the bottle and come running.

My dog Archie's hair coat never looked great. Although a Wire-Haired Terrier, he had the type of coat that hovers between curly and straight and stiff and soft, and it grew longer than it should. He always looked like he needed grooming, even after he'd just been trimmed. Furthermore he smelled. Before I added healthful oils to his diet, he often smelled like a combination of old running shoes and rancid fat. After adding those oils, he still looked in need of a good coiffing, but the odor disappeared, and his hair coat became much softer. If the smell and hair-coat problems were due only to allergenic food ingredients, the hypoallergenic diet should have helped. In his case, it took adding oils to his hypoallergenic diet to solve his stinky, stiff fur problem. Omega oils helped Archie's skin clear up, just as had occurred with the skin of the dog given the "wonder skin supplement" and the skins of the rats in the essential fatty acid experiments.

Dry, itchy skin from a deficiency of fats and oils may be prone to allergic reactions, whereas skin bathed in the right amount of fats and oils may be more resistant to inflammation from food allergens or the environment. I speak from firsthand experience because it seems that no matter what type of allergies dogs have, adding omega and monounsaturated fats to their diet seems to bring some relief. Even if the skin looks relatively healthy it still can be prone to bouts of inflammation and infections due to allergies. I myself now take fish-oil capsules, and I make certain that I use products with omega oils and less saturated fat. Experience has been my teacher; it's a lesson I share with my canine friends.

The Great Healthy Teeth and Gums Charade

Once my clients start their dogs on a non-allergenic regimen, the next question is usually about alternatives to the beef bones and biscuits that they used to keep their dogs' teeth and gums in great shape. Actually I have a lot to say on the subject, and it may surprise you.

First, many of my clients think that biscuits and kibble are better for dental health than canned food. I disagree. In fact, dental problems seem to be associated more with breeds, and I think almost all dogs are born with the genetics for either good or bad teeth and gums. In my practice, the toy breeds have many more dental problems than the other breeds, regardless of their diet. Some individual animals in every breed may need routine veterinary dental care. Halitosis hounds have a tendency to develop a lot of tartar, inflamed gums and putrid breath. After scaling and polishing under anesthesia, brushing and home dental care can help prevent further build-up of tartar and the associated inflamed gums.

As for the incessant biscuit question, I will answer it with a question of my own. Would it help your teeth and gums for you to chew on a stale cookie every day? I hate to repeat myself, but a dry, high-carbohydrate cookie may not be the answer for sound teeth and gums. Furthermore, I've fed my dogs canned food for 10 years and see less tartar buildup than took place with previous dry-food diets.

> *I hate to repeat myself, but a dry, high-carbohydrate cookie may not be the answer for sound teeth and gums. Furthermore, I've fed my dogs canned food for 10 years and see less tartar buildup than took place with previous dry-food diets.*

What do you think a wolf does to clean his teeth? He doesn't floss with a porcupine quill. Most dogs intuitively know the answer to this question and are often scolded for doing it. Dogs love to chew. We can use that inner drive to help keep their teeth clean. Wolves keep their teeth clean by chewing on the bones of prey animals. In that tradition, you can give your dog raw or frozen chicken thighs, smoked pork bones or beef knucklebones, and they'll gnaw the tartar away.

> *Wolves keep their teeth clean by chewing on the bones of prey animals. In that tradition, you can give your dog raw or frozen chicken thighs, smoked pork bones or beef knucklebones, and they'll gnaw the tartar away.*

But wait, you say, hasn't Dr. Greg been preaching this whole time to avoid beef in the diet? I have. But I've also found an exception. Raw beef knucklebones do not seem to cause the allergic reactions and skin problems that beef products and meat frequently will. These large bones have almost no meat on them. They have small amounts of ligaments and cartilage that we call gristle. Chewing and eating these natural products will make many dogs happy. They will chew off the gristle and spend long periods trying to lick and gnaw their way to the inside of the bone containing the nutrient-rich marrow that contains very healthful fats. In fact, when I give each of my dogs a bone to chew on, they get a glazed, far-away look in their eyes and chew for hours. This reminds me of the chewing scenes on television nature programs whereupon the predators are pictured contentedly masticating the bones of the kill. As I watch my dogs expertly turn and gnaw the large, *raw* knucklebones, I imagine them hearing the distant call of their ancestors. This is the real bone therapy.

`Dem Bones and Other Chews

Before you rush out to purchase bones, be aware that bones can also be the most dangerous food item you give your dog. You need to select the *right* bones. You also need to know how your dog will handle a bone. Some dogs will devour small, cooked bones, and these *bone plugs* can block the intestine and cause major medical or surgical problems. <u>Dogs must chew bones, not eat them. They should never be allowed to swallow bones whole or in large pieces.</u> If you choose to feed your dog bones, large raw or smoked ones are best. Big leg bones such as knucklebones and hocks are difficult to crack, split or swallow in chunks. In contrast, ribs or T-bones (even raw) can be dangerous to feed because almost all dogs devour them quickly and can develop intestinal blockage or severe constipation, and when cooked they are hard and brittle and likely to break and splinter when chewed.

> "*Dogs must chew bones, not eat them. They should never be allowed to swallow bones whole or in large pieces. If you choose to feed your dog bones, large raw or smoked ones are best.*"

Barbecued, baked or fried chicken leg bones also can splinter and cause damage, but *raw* chicken bones (or those simmered in a crock pot for 10 to 12 hours) are softer and safer. Pluis Davern has fed her dogs raw chicken with the bones included for at least 10 years without any problems. After she started feeding that diet, her dogs rarely needed dental care.

Ultimately, the decision to give your dog a bone comes down to the kind of chewer it is. Believe it or not, some dogs want nothing to do with a bone. These non-chewing dogs with tartar build-up will require medical treatment from your veterinarian. Other dogs do not want to chew bones; they want to gulp them down. <u>If your dog is a gulper and swallower, the risks from chewing bones outweigh the benefits.</u> If your dog chews on a bone for a while but then digs up all the flowers in your planter box to bury it, bones may not be worth the frustration and mess.

> " *If your dog is a gulper and swallower, the risks from chewing bones outweigh the benefits.* "

Dogs that seem to enjoy the activity and take their time chewing are the best candidates for bone therapy. I buy smoked pork bones or raw knucklebones and, depending on the size, hacksaw them into pieces (you can often ask the butcher do it for you) and divide the pieces among my dogs. The size of the bone that I give each dog is relative to the size of its jaws. Maisy, my little dog, gets a much smaller piece of bone than my 90-pound Lab, Tucker. I let them chew on the bones for a few hours then, if there are any pieces left, I store them in the freezer for next time. *I try to remember to offer bones every two to three weeks.*

The Pig's Ear Caution

My dogs enjoy a good chew on pigs' ears. Pigskin and pigs' ears may also be a good choice for a chewy treat although I've had a few clients tell me that their dog vomited after eating pigs' ears. My biggest concern is for the dogs that swallow the ears in large pieces because that can lead to intestinal blockages. The bottom line is this: You have to be cautious when you give your dogs stuff to chew. If they swallow big pieces of anything, it can lead to medical problems requiring surgical remedies.

Another chew treat I give my dogs is frozen chicken thighs. In fact, I gave them each a frozen chicken thigh as I wrote this paragraph. Tucker crushes and finishes the small "pupsickle" in a few minutes, but Archie and Maisy may take anywhere from 10 to 15 minutes to chew and eat it. Frozen chicken is good for their teeth and their general well being. The small bones are raw, soft and easy to crush and digest. *Do not be alarmed when you discover the poop is much paler or almost white the next couple of days.*

Some worry about the risk of *Salmonella* infection in their dogs or family when raw chicken is fed. The risk is small but there are precautions you should take: You should wash your hands thoroughly. Very young children and adults with health problems, such as a compromised immune system, probably should avoid handling raw chicken. You might also want to avoid letting your dog lick your face right after he's eaten raw chicken. For myself, I'm more focused on the fact that once the frozen pieces thaw, they look pretty disgusting. My dogs like to eat the bloody piece of meat on the furniture they think they own. Thank goodness we have leather

Photo by Rosemary Rideout

couches. You might want to have your dogs take their treats outside to avoid seeing the carnage.

Meaty-Wheaty Treats Are Doggie Junk Food

All dogs love to eat anything in addition to their normal food. Being social creatures of habit, they look forward to the treats that are given every morning and evening. In fact, dogs will learn our movements or the phrases we use that are associated with the act of going to the treat location.

The treat sequence in our house goes like this: The word "potty" gets them to jump from the couches and head for the sliding-glass door. They then hurry to the potty area in the backyard and quickly pee so they can run back to the kitchen where Lonna is digging into the chicken-and-rice treat bag for their evening snack. You'd think those treats were the best-tasting food on Earth. I have nibbled on the treats, and they taste like a thick, bland, stale biscuit. My dogs have a different opinion. I assumed that dogs like the crunchiness of the biscuits, but some dogs seem to inhale them with just one or two quick bites. The type of treat does not seem to be as important as the anticipated reward. A client that trains search-and-rescue dogs uses the toys her service dogs love for a reward instead of treats. Nearly all dogs will come to recognize any treat sequence and react just like Pavlov's dogs.

The traditional dog treat is a crunchy biscuit made with wheat flour and meat, conveniently packaged, and designed to be offered between feedings. The variety of sizes, textures, ingredients, colors and fillings of treats available at pet stores, or in pet food aisles at the supermarket, illustrates how big a business treats are for commercial dog food companies.

But remember, for our purposes a treat is only as good as its ingredients. Wheat gluten, wheat flour, corn and meat by-products from beef are usually the ingredients responsible for most of the allergic symptoms in pets. When dogs with skin, ear, stomach and bowel problems (even mild seizures) come in to our clinic, I always review the types of treats that the ailing one is eating. I often find the allergy symptoms started with the purchase and feeding of a new type of meaty-wheaty treat.

Carly, what should we have today? Green beans and deli turkey? Zucchini casserole? Frozen chicken thighs? Egg yolk? Carrot? Maybe some leftover salmon or a few shrimp?

If your dog has allergy symptoms or is over-weight, I do not recommend calorie-dense, meaty-wheaty treats. Treats made with wheat, beef and even corn ingredients will often bring on itching, hives, inflamed ears, vomiting, diarrhea or seizures. If your dog has allergy symptoms and you feel a need to feed a biscuit, try a treat made from healthful hypoallergenic ingredients.

> *If your dog has allergy symptoms and you feel a need to feed a biscuit, try a treat made from healthful hypoallergenic ingredients.*

The year that I graduated and started my career in veterinary medicine was a rough one. Although vets fresh out of school are well educated, they lack the perspective gleaned from years of practice. Good diagnoses are reached based on both education and practical experience; it just takes more energy and time when you're new at it.

I came home one day, certain my career was over because a case had not gone well. I grabbed a beer from the fridge and moped at the kitchen table. I felt hungry and saw a foil package with a picture of jerky on the front. I ripped off the top, grabbed a piece and ate it. The taste seemed a little off, and the jerky was softer than normal and easy to bite through, but my depression over the day's events clouded my judgment. I kept munching on the jerky as I reviewed my day and what I could have done differently. I heard the front door and greeted Lonna with a long face and told her what had happened. Then I added that I didn't like the taste of the jerky I had been eating. She seemed sympathetic, but then started giggling. I asked her what she found so funny about my horrid experience. Looking at the empty foil package she blurted out, "I'm sorry you had a bad day, but you've just finished all of Sadie's jerky treats!"

Making Sense of Nutritional Chart Language

I strolled through a major, pet food store recently comparing label presentations to ingredient lists. The labels on the front proudly displayed graphics and words of chicken, rice, vegetables, fish and lamb, but in most cases the ingredients listed on the back labels contained some form of the beef, wheat and corn I try to avoid. Here's one giveaway: The labels on the front of the can or bag that contain words such as *dinner, formula, gravy* and *mix* usually have wheat, beef and/or corn among the ingredients listed on the back label. Beef is also listed as meat, meat by-products or liver.

As I was scanning the cans, I wondered why beef had so many other descriptive terms. My only conclusion is that beef's identity is hidden in some foods to foster the promotion of other varieties of protein. This makes it easier to use multiple products chosen for their low cost and ready availability. Beef or lamb lungs; spleen; kidney; brain; liver; blood; bone; partially defatted, low-temperature fatty tissue; and stomachs and intestines freed of their contents are more cost-effective than beaks and feet alone. The truth is, there's just enough chicken in a beef by-product mix to allow the manufacturer (following the percentage rules of labeling) to call it chicken and rice.

> "The truth is, there's just enough chicken in a beef by-product mix to allow the manufacturer (following the percentage rules of labeling) to call it chicken and rice."

In case you're wondering about the labeling laws, at the back of this book (Appendix B) I've included a nice summary written by a veterinarian from the Food and Drug Administration about the four labeling rules for the Association of American Feed Control Officials (AAFCO). Even that well-written summary needs to be read several times to be fully understood, but it comes down to this: *If you are avoiding allergenic ingredients, do not rely on the descriptive label on the front.* You must read the actual list of ingredients to know exactly what proteins and carbohydrates are in a particular dog food. Deciphering an ingredients list requires you to understand the language of nutrition, which consists of ingredients, preservatives and nutrients. Let me give you a crash course.

A food *ingredient* is the type of protein (meat), carbohydrate (grain or vegetable) or fat that is contained in the meal. Let's start by focusing on the meat or domestic, food-animal *protein* ingredient. The most commonly used meats, in order of popularity, are beef, chicken, lamb, duck or their by-products. AAFCO defines meat *by-products* as:

> *...the non-rendered clean parts, other than meat, derived from slaughtered mammals. It includes, but is not limited to, lungs, spleen, kidneys, brain, livers, blood, bone, partially defatted low temperature fatty tissue, and stomachs and intestines freed of their contents. It does not include hair, horns, teeth and hooves. It shall be suitable for use in animal food. If it bears a name descriptive of its kind, it must correspond thereto.*

While I'll admit that the AAFCO description does not sound very appetizing, the ancestors of our pets ate their share of all of the above. The animal parts listed here are perfectly acceptable as dog food, even though they sound awful. If you want your pet to have human-grade chicken instead, you'll either have to buy it at the market and make your own dog food, find a dog food that states right on the label that it contains human-grade chicken, or share part of your food.

The next category of food ingredient in dog food is *carbohydrates*. Canned food and dry food (or kibble) usually contain between 30 percent and 70 percent carbohydrates, respectively. These ingredients are listed as "grains or vegetables" and usually include wheat, corn, rice, potato or carrots. The traditional definition of a vegetable is "the edible part of a plant," as opposed to fruit, which is the sweet, fleshy, reproductive, seed-containing part of a plant. This is why tomatoes are often called fruit.

You may wonder why I mention tomatoes. You may also wonder if they are good for dogs. My Golden Retriever Teddy used to carry tennis balls around in his mouth 24/7. When he walked up without a ball clamped in his jaws, it always took a second or two to figure out what was missing. He even tried to carry a tomato on occasion. Lonna and I started growing a garden several years ago, and both of us eagerly waited for those sweet, juicy, homegrown tomatoes to ripen. "Tonight's the night," I told Lonna one morning as we surveyed the tomato patch. "We're going to have our first tomatoes of the season."

When I came home from work, I eagerly went to the garden to pick our succulent appetizers. To my dismay, the ripest tomatoes were gone. Naturally, I accused Lonna of being greedy and not sharing our bounty. But she had nothing to do with the crime. The next few tomatoes ripened then disappeared like before. I began accusing our friends, neighbors, aliens and whomever else came to mind to explain this mystery. One day I was working in the garden when Teddy came right over to the tomato plant, smelled a few of the tomatoes, then picked and ate the ripest one. The brazen tomato thief did not take very long to eat it either—or add any salt, for that matter. All I could do was laugh and put a small fence around the garden. Since I caught the crafty carnivore sneaking a veggie, I tried feeding him different fruits and vegetables. He loved apples, bananas, cherries, peaches, carrots and, of course, tomatoes.

I wondered if other dogs relished veggies and fruit as much. One night Lonna and I picked green beans and tossed them into a colander lying on the grass between us. Maisy moseyed over, smelled them until she found a young, tender, sweet one. She picked it out, put her paw on one end and deftly chewed off the opposite end. Her actions were deliberate and seemed almost practiced, even though she had had few opportunities to learn the art of bean eating. Her behavior must be something included in the standard canine software. *The take-home lesson is that a diet from more food sources is more likely to satisfy any individual's needs.*

Archie, on the other hand, stuck to his meat diet. He'd smell any veggie or fruit offering then turn away. Tucker will always eat a bit of any offering because he is a Lab and desperately wants to be a good boy. This is a good experiment for you to try at home. See which fruits and veggies your dogs like to eat; they may surprise you.

> *See which fruits and veggies your dogs like to eat; they may surprise you.*

Back to our label reading: *Fats and oils* may be listed as coming from a particular domestic, food-animal source, such as tallow, lard or oil (from cow, pig, sheep, chicken, duck, turkey, salmon, etc.). They may also be from a plant source, such as corn, soy, canola or other oilseed plants.

Meats (proteins), grains and vegetables (carbohydrates) and fats and oils are usually listed on the first two lines of the label. The vitamins, minerals and preservatives follow. For some heavily preserved foods, the chemical list can be quite long. To illustrate how this works, I have copied several ingredient labels so you can follow along. Let's start with an easy one. Halo's Spot's Stew is a nutritious food that

I've given to my own dogs and recommended to my clients for years. It's ingredients are: Chicken broth, chicken, carrots, celery, yellow squash, zucchini, chicken liver, pasta, green peas, green beans, turkey, calcium citrate, barley, oats, dicalcium phosphate, soy sauce, dried kelp, garlic, zinc gluconate, ascorbic acid, copper gluconate.

We might as well be reading the label on a can of soup. The list of wholesome ingredients does not include three lines of preservative and stabilizer lingo. That and the fact that it has no beef/beef by-products or obvious wheat or corn glutens (the pasta is made with quinoa flour but the soy sauce may have wheat) makes Spot's Stew an excellent choice for dogs with allergic symptoms.

Let's try another one. The ingredients are: Ground yellow corn, chicken by-product meal, corn gluten meal, whole wheat flour, animal fat preserved with mixed-tocopherols (form of Vitamin E), rice flour, beef, soy flour, sugar, sorbitol, tricalcium phosphate, water, salt, phosphoric acid, animal digest, potassium chloride, dicalcium phosphate, sorbic acid (a preservative), L-Lysine monohydrochloride, dried peas, dried carrots, calcium carbonate, calcium propionate (a preservative), choline chloride, added color (Yellow 5, Red 40, Yellow 6, Blue 2), DL-Methionine, Vitamin E supplement, zinc sulfate, ferrous sulfate, Vitamin A supplement, manganese sulfate, niacin, Vitamin B-12 supplement, calcium pantothenate, riboflavin supplement, copper sulfate, biotin, garlic oil, thiamine hydrochloride, pyridoxine hydrochloride, thiamine mononitrate, folic acid, Vitamin D-3 supplement, menadione sodium bisulfite complex (source of Vitamin K activity), calcium iodate, sodium selenite.

Chicken and rice? There's more corn than chicken in this formula.

Quite different, isn't it. Actually it's a typical ingredient label on a bag or can of dog food or package of treats. After the third line, the words on the label sound more like a high-school chemistry report than something you'd want your best friend to eat. Now you have to figure out if this is something Rex should eat. Let's take the list apart: Ingredients are always listed in order of the highest to lowest percentage. In most commercial dog foods the percentage of car-

> ## Ingredients are always listed in order of the highest to lowest percentage.

bohydrates are usually the highest, and sure enough, in our example ground yellow corn is first. Whole-wheat flour and rice flour are also among the top six ingredients. This diet would not work for those dogs allergic to wheat or corn. Remember, if you are trying to figure out what ingredients your dog is allergic to, the rule of thumb is the fewer ingredients the better.

Next we'll check the meat and protein ingredients: chicken by-product meal, corn gluten meal, beef, soy flour and animal digest. Remember the difference between the label and the ingredients list; this food is advertised as a chicken-type dog food, but it has several known allergens as proteins, including corn gluten, beef and an unknown mix of critters called "animal digest." Chicken by-product meal is not breasts and thighs, but at least we know it's from a chicken.

If your dog gets nauseous, develops ear problems, gets the runs or stinks up the house after eating beef products, this food could be a problem. This is particularly important in dogs with intestinal problems and pancreatitis that can be triggered by diets containing beef and beef fat. When we check the fats, we find animal fat preserved with mixed-tocopherols (form of Vitamin E). This could be a mix of beef, chicken or other available fat. Again, if your dog has allergic tendencies, it is best to know exactly which animal fats he is consuming.

All this goes to show that just because the label on the front says chicken and rice, that's no guarantee that the ingredients are free of beef, wheat, corn, lamb or other proteins and carbohydrates. You can admire the pictures and graphics on the front of a bag or can of food, but to know what you're actually feeding your dog READ THE INGREDIENTS ON THE BACK. And even when you read the label, you must have a general idea of the ingredients you want, or do not want, in your dog's diet. With two pieces of information— 1) what kinds of food are best for your dog and 2) what's actually in the commercial dog food you've selected—you can make good decisions about what products are best for your dog.

> *You can admire the pictures and graphics on the front of a bag or can of food, but to know what you're actually feeding your dog READ THE INGREDIENTS ON THE BACK.*

Let's try one more. The ingredients are: Chicken broth, chicken, beef by-products, chicken by-products, beef liver, brewers rice, chicken by-product meal, dried beet pulp, guar gum, titanium dioxide, flax meal, calcium sulfate, sodium tripolyphosphate, potassium chloride, brewers dried yeast, dried egg product, vitamins (Vitamin E supplement, ascorbic acid, thiamine mononitrate (source of vitamin B1), Vitamin A acetate, calcium pantothenate, biotin, Vitamin B12 supplement, niacin, riboflavin supplement (source of vitamin B2), inositol, pyridoxine hydrochloride (source of Vitamin B6), Vitamin D3 supplement, folic acid), salt, carrageenan, cassia gum, choline chloride, minerals (ferrous sulfate, zinc oxide, manganese sulfate, copper sulfate, manganous oxide, potassium iodide, cobalt carbonate).

The Elimination Diet

If your dog has allergies, your first task is to identify the source of its problem. Start with a chicken-and-rice diet; make sure there are no beef, wheat or corn products among the ingredients in the food, treats or chews. If that does not make your pet more comfortable, try duck and potato, lamb and rice, or foods with novel proteins, such as venison or fish with rice or vegetables. This is not an all-inclusive list. Other healthful, hypoallergenic, dog food formulas include novel proteins such as turkey, bison, even kangaroo, and other carbohydrates (e.g., barley and sweet potatoes).

If your dog does not have any allergies, the type of ingredients may not be as important to you as the quality. Again the fewer ingredients listed on the back label, the better. Higher-quality foods may cost a little more, but if your dog feels better with the meat and carbohydrate ingredients in the diet, and you can live with the price, then you have a winner.

This label is from a dog food product advertised as a chicken-and-rice blend. Remember, if any of the terms *blend, gravy, platter, dinner, entrée, mix, formula,* or any other savory adjective are on the front label, you will always find some combination of meat and grain ingredients listed on the back label. On the above label, chicken is listed first, but other proteins such as beef by-products, beef liver and dried egg products follow. Brewer's rice is listed as the sole carbohydrate, and no other grain. Even though the label says chicken and rice, a dog that is sensitive to beef could have real problems with this diet.

You should now have a better idea of what to look for. Armed with the knowledge of what is best for your dog, you can shop smarter.

Inexpensive Commercial Dog Foods... Don't Let Your Dog Pay the Price

When I ask my clients what diet they are feeding their dog, most reply by telling me the brand name of the food, to which I have to confess that I'm not familiar with every one of the multitudes of brands and their corresponding ingredients. What I really want to know is what *type* of food they are feeding. Is it a dry food similar in composition to an ancient cookie? Is the food in a plastic or foil package that has the consistency of a moist meatloaf? Or maybe it's a moist, soupy, stew consistency and comes in a can. I also want to know about the *ingredients*. What kind of meat does the diet contain? What sort of carbohydrate? I also ask about the *category* of diet.

There are many categories of dog diets on the market that can make selection very confusing. There are life-stage diets, breed-specific diets and medical diets. In truth, I am not a firm believer in requiring a whole slew of special diets for one species. If the same principles were applied to humans, a typical dinner conversation might be, "Honey, the Martinez's are coming for dinner, and I see adult formula and children 12-18 growth plus, but we're out of the young children 7-12 developmental formula. Oh, and the developmental formula needs to be the Asian diet for little Jennifer since she was adopted in China." Right about now you're probably wondering if there are magical ingredients for each life stage or breed that we should know about. Not really. Let me explain.

Medical diets have ingredients that are combined to help treat and control medical conditions. Allergy diets, for example, are hypoallergenic and made with non-allergenic or novel meats or proteins and non-allergenic carbohydrates. Urinary diets and urinary-stone diets are mixes of low-ash ingredients formulated to reduce the amount of calcium and phosphorus the body has to eliminate in the urine to help prevent crystals and stones from forming. Diabetes diets reduce the amount of carbohydrate and increase the fiber; intestinal- and pancreas-formulated diets are often low fat, hypoallergenic and also higher in fiber. Medical diets help decrease discomfort, symptoms or problems associated with medical conditions. They're based on ingredients known to be helpful with each condition. My only problem is that most dry food weight-reduction, diabetes and urinary formulas are using a mix of dry, high-carbohydrate nutrients that may be a factor in causing the problem in the first place. Ironic, isn't it? A healthier diet with a more natural, moister and hypoallergenic mix of ingredients may prevent the need for medical diets.

Joint-health diets have glucosamine, chondroitin and MSM added. The same ingredients are found in pill, liquid or powder forms at many supermarkets, pharmacies and vitamin stores and you can, with a quick flip of the wrist, easily add these supplements to the food. In fact, those same ingredients are also found in chicken gristle, shrimp tails and chicken sternums that you may not want to eat but your dog might gobble up if given the chance. If your dog is overweight or has other medical problems, it might be better to start with a lower-calorie, canned food with healthful, hypoallergenic ingredients then add some glucosamine, chondroitin, MSM, gristle, cartilage or shrimp tails.

Weight-loss diets for dogs often mirror the popular human notion that it is fat, and not the large portions of processed carbohydrate, that contributes to weight gain. These diets further decrease the already critically low levels of fat in the typical dog diet—an ingredient that did not cause the problem in the first place. A dry, high-carbohydrate, low-fat diet may actually lead to more health problems than it helps. *A diet with more moisture and fewer calories per serving—such as a smaller serving of dry food*

I Can't Say Enough About the Great Treat Bamboozle (cont.)

feeding of treats is usually more of an emotional bonding habit than a nutritional necessity. Better choices: *Hypoallergenic and more nutritious types of commercial treats made with chicken and rice, chicken and vegetables, or other non-allergenic combinations.* Best choices: *Baby carrots, pieces of deli meat, healthful leftovers or scraps, turkey hotdogs, green beans and even shrimp.*

How to Feed a Puppy

Puppy foods usually have a little more protein, and the kibbles are smaller and easier for puppies to chew. Senior diets have less protein and, in this food as well, the kibbles are small and easier to chew. Are the differences in these diets critical? I personally don't think so. When people have two or three dogs, it gets expensive buying puppy, adult and senior diets. Besides, the truth is every dog will want to eat every other dog's food, and I don't recommend the job of being the food police to your dogs. If you have several dogs, including a puppy, you can feed them all adult dog food. That includes the puppy. Just give the puppy a small piece of extra protein daily, such as chicken, turkey, fish or pork, to make up for the needed additional protein missing in the adult formula. And there are healthier ways too to feed a senior-citizen canine other than a stale, boring, low-protein, cookie-like diet. You can feed a hypoallergenic, canned diet with chicken and rice or chicken and vegetables and supplement the diet with high-quality, healthful human food ingredients. Or you can cook for your aged pet.

supplemented with chicken broth and canned green beans, good healthful canned food, homemade food or raw diets—would be a much healthier way for your pet to lose weight. Remember, kibble is the most popular type of dog food because it is economical and easy to feed; not because it's the best choice for your pet.

> " *A healthier diet with a more natural and hypoallergenic mix of ingredients may prevent the need for medical diets.* "

The Case for Canned Food

Canned food has the same meat and grain by-products as kibble or dry food but is mixed and processed differently. There is a lot more water and fewer carbohydrates and preservatives in the mixture. The process evolved from the canning of meats, grains and vegetables that were not destined for immediate use on our tables. Canned dog food has a long shelf life, but beware: When it's opened it will grow mold faster than any bread ever could. A time or two I have left half of an opened can on top of the fridge and found it after we were alerted by the odor. To avoid this nauseating experience, you need to use the whole can in one feeding or refrigerate the leftover contents for the next feeding.

Unfortunately, canned dog food has a public-relations problem. Many of my clients have negative impressions of dog food in cans. This may have started way back when horsemeat was regularly used for dog food. Some clients think it's "too rich" and causes diarrhea. And, of course, many are convinced that kibble is necessary for the health of their dog's teeth. Ah, such are the urban legends that abound. Don't let any of these beliefs deter you from trying this healthful type of food.

What does "too rich" mean anyway? The phrase usually applies to chocolate or fat, and we know dogs can't eat chocolate. When a sauce is too rich, it usually contains a lot of butter or fat. Today regulations require labels on canned dog food to state the nutrients they contain. Most canned dog foods contain between 10 percent and 25 percent fat. That amount of fat is not too rich.

The fact is, diarrhea is usually the result of *ingredients* that do not agree with the individual. In the case of dogs, diarrhea is usually caused by an allergy to beef, wheat, corn or other ingredients. The softer consistency due to the water content of canned food will not lead to diarrhea. This would be the same as saying we would get diarrhea every time we ate soup or stew. In truth, the moister a food is the less work the body has to do to digest it. Canned food should be easier on the digestive system as long as it contains the right ingredients. And one more complaint: Lonna hates the texture, smell and obnoxious sucking sound of canned food as it plops in the bowl. Manufacturers, any suggestions?

> "*Canned food should be easier on the digestive system as long as it contains the right ingredients.*"

Schools of Food...er, Thought

The majority of dog owners are confused about all the nutritional claims made by the commercial, dog food industry as well as the recommendations by veterinarians, breeders, relatives and friends about what and what not to feed their pets. The choices fall into three schools of thought.

Commercial Manufacturers. The first school of thought suggests that commercial dog food is so complete—and the balance so delicate—that the simple addition of a scrap of chicken or a piece of carrot may contribute to medical problems or nutritional deficiencies. Most dog food companies and veterinarians belong to this school and champion feeding only a high-quality brand of complete-and-balanced dog food. I myself was similarly brainwashed in vet school and in the early days of my practice, but I'm recovering and now offer my pets healthful, non-allergenic people food whenever I want to.

Biologically Appropriate Raw Food (BARF) Diet. Another school of thought recommends the diet of the wolf and advocates the feeding of raw muscle and organs to our pets. Since our dogs are genetically 99.8 percent wolf, this seems a reasonable approach. This is feeding your dog's inner wolf in the extreme. Even though many raw diets contain beef, owners that feed raw products as part of the BARF diet report that their dogs look and feel much better. It makes me wonder if my patients are allergic to beef, or just to the way we process it.

Raw diets are controversial because of the problems of storage and processing. Raw meat has the potential to be contaminated with *E. coli* bacteria. This is even more of a problem today than in the past due to our current, high-density, animal-agriculture practices; similarly it's far easier to catch a cold in a crowded subway than it is in a bookstore on a weekday afternoon. The same principle applies if a sick cow is crowded into a feedlot with thousands of other animals; the bugs just naturally spread more rapidly and easily. A bug such as *E. coli* may be passed from the "graduating class" to the "freshman class" by contact. These bacteria are passed from cow to cow and continually bathed with antibiotics until it becomes resistant to most drugs. The industry is very good about restricting antibiotic usage and keeping processing plants clean, but outbreaks are inevitable. Inherent in this controversy is that the potential for human and/or canine infection exists. I have no experience feeding commercial raw diets and am not aware of any medical problems resulting from their use in my patients. If you are comfortable with the issues, and your dog does not have problems with beef, raw diets may make a lot of sense. The wolf has survived for millions of years eating in just that fashion.

Dog Food Feeding Trials: Understanding AAFCO Standard Nutrient Profiles (cont.)

to complete the feeding trial while maintaining their weight, and must pass veterinary exams and blood tests.

It's good to know that commercial dog diets must meet standards…and yet. As we now know, obesity, skin, ear, stomach and intestinal problems plague many dogs eating high-carbohydrate, dry food—as do the allergenic wheat, beef and corn ingredients in many commercial foods. My concern is that these issues may not surface immediately; it may take a few years for a problem to become acute and chronic. Also some breeds are more susceptible than others. In order for these feeding trials to be more helpful, they need to include many different breeds and address health issues with certain ingredients. Unfortunately, the AAFCO requirements and feeding trials leave me with more questions than answers. What I do know is that the way we feed our dogs causes mild to severe problems in about 30 percent of my patients, and if you factor in obesity and dry skin, that number is much higher.

Human-Grade, Natural and Holistic Options. Holistic, natural and organic dog foods are wholesome offerings with a minimum of additives and preservatives. They are probably the most healthful...and, in some ways, the most controversial. The meats, grains and vegetables may be human-grade ingredients. Non-food, chemical additives, such as preservatives and food coloring, in commercial dog food may help cause immunity problems, tumors, illness and disease. Personally I believe that the blame for these diseases must be shared with dry, high-calorie, fat-deficient, allergenic diets. Holistic and natural diets, however, might help dogs with severe allergies that require the absolute minimum of allergens in their food. These diets require a higher grade of food product and packaging and usually carry a higher price. But you have to

remember that even expensive food is usually cheaper than vet bills.

The alternative to buying a commercial organic food is to make it yourself. Home-prepared dog food is a healthful mix of human-grade ingredients. You can make batches of food the way my friend Al Howard does by cooking two, whole chickens along with some carrots, squash and green beans in the crock pot until the meat falls off the softened bones (10 to 12 hours). He refrigerates the mixture and feeds portions of it daily. You can also feed healthful, non-allergenic people food such as chicken, turkey, pork, fish, carrots, squash, potatoes and rice from your own prepared meals. As long as the meal does not contain big pieces of whole onion, garlic or an over-abundance of spices, it can be safe to share. (Note: A medium-size onion is actually toxic to a dog and may cause problems.)

Raw Chicken Bones for Clean Teeth (cont.)

Since that day, neither Pluis nor I have had any problems with Salmonella or splintering chicken bone injuries. However, feeding bones, just as feeding of commercial, raw-food diets, carries a small risk of infection and injury from the bones. So you'll have to use your own judgment.

When I tell people about the option to add people food, many look up with a sheepish grin and then reveal their dark secret about already feeding their dog people food. *Your dog should thrive on and enjoy this diet as long as you do not feed ingredients toxic or allergenic to dogs and don't overdo on the carbs.* Exercise caution when dogs have medical conditions such as pancreatitis, diabetes and intestinal problems. Always start out with very small trial pieces of any new ingredient to test your dog's tolerance for the food. And if you decide to supplement commercial dog food with people food, factor the table scraps into the overall daily allotment so you are not overfeeding.

Cooking for Rex

Homemade dog food is a lot like canned dog food, only you know exactly what's in it because you select the ingredients. Commercial diets, on the other hand, contain parts that are left over from processing animals for human consumption. As part of my effort to give my dogs variety, I make their food a couple times a month. I select good, healthful, human-grade ingredients, but I know some people who will only give their dogs organic.

Making your own dog food is not as convenient as opening a bag or can, but it's not all that time-consuming either. Actually, it's fun, and you can get the kids involved. It takes about five minutes to prepare the ingredients, and then you leave them to cook in a crock pot for 10 to 12 hours. It's a great way to treat your dog. And if you want Rex to eat human-grade, high-quality dog food, making your own is much more economical. A couple of warnings: Store your homemade dog food in the refrigerator. And if you decide to make some food ahead (more than you can use in a couple of days), you'll need to freeze it or it will spoil. Okay, here's my secret recipe:

1 whole chicken (4 1/2 to 8 pounds, really depends on the size of your crock pot)

2 medium potatoes (you can substitute a yam)

1 bag frozen green beans (you can substitute a can or use fresh in season)

Enough water to cover ingredients (1 – 2 cups)

Put chicken (and neck, liver and gizzards) in crock pot. Wash and cut potatoes into quarters and add to pot. Add bag of green beans. Add water. Cover and cook. I start my crock pot on high, but after about an hour (or once the ingredients are bubbling) I turn it down to low and leave it to simmer for 10 to 12 hours. When the chicken mixture is done, I bone the chicken (reserving bones for later use) and combine all ingredients in a large bowl. Now for the bones—when I cook them this long, they are soft, particularly the ends. I pull ends off and add these soft knuckle joints, along with their gristle and marrow, to my mixture. Then I chop using a stick blender or food processor. I divide into plastic containers and store either in the refrigerator or freezer.

If you want to cook organic or add rice (cooked separately), you certainly can.

> *"Always start out with very small trial pieces of any new ingredient to test your dog's tolerance for the food. And if you decide to supplement commercial dog food with people food, factor the table scraps into the overall daily allotment so you are not overfeeding."*

When I tell people to avoid feeding beef, wheat and corn, some inevitably reply that they never feed table scraps, assuming that I am talking about scraps or leftovers, not ingredients. I look them right in the eye and tell them that it is okay to feed people food as long as they follow the rules. Then I explain: "Beef and wheat are ingredients to avoid feeding your dog in all commercial diets, home-prepared foods, treats, chews and when giving scraps." I follow with, "You can safely give your dog healthful, human food such as chicken, turkey, ham, eggs, fish, shrimp, carrots and green beans." *And now I'll remind you: Beef scraps include hamburger, steak, tri-tip, roast, meatloaf and especially the fat cut off of a steak.* Feeding any of these may be followed by inflamed ears, hotspots, seizures, nausea, vomiting, diarrhea or a hospital stay with a diagnosis of acute pancreatitis.

The other night Lonna and I were enjoying some shrimp and vegetables. The shrimp were fried in garlic and olive oil with their tails on, so I made a nice little pile of tails on my plate. After we finished, I mentioned to Lonna that the glucosamine supplement she was taking listed shrimp as the source. "I bet these tails would be good for the dogs," I said as I threw a few on the floor. All three dogs relished the flavorful, crunchy treats and suffered no undesirable after effects. About three days later, I was foraging in the refrigerator and found the rest of the shrimp we hadn't eaten for dinner. They looked and smelled fine so I split them up between the dogs—tails and all. This

The Chocolate Rule: Never, Ever Feed Your Dog
Chocolate Before Church (or any other time!)

Chocolate always tops the A list for foods toxic to dogs. I've made lots of dogs throw up (preventative medicine) after they ate some, and I've seen a few dogs with the jitters due to dark-chocolate ingestion. But of all my experiences, I will never forget Abby.

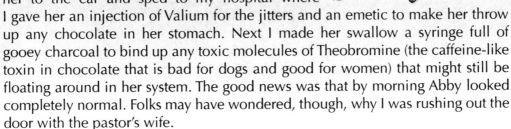

Our friends Andy and Lynn invited us to their church for a Christmas musical. I hadn't even relaxed in my seat before the pastor's wife rushed up to me and said that we had to leave. Their son had just called in a panic because their Golden Retriever Abby was acting extremely peculiar. We rushed to the house to find red-and-green foil wrappers all over the floor and an empty condiment bowl on the coffee table. When we entered the kitchen, there stood the perpetrator, trembling uncontrollably from the effects of the caffeine-like drug in the chocolate. I snatched her up, carried her to the car and sped to my hospital where I gave her an injection of Valium for the jitters and an emetic to make her throw up any chocolate in her stomach. Next I made her swallow a syringe full of gooey charcoal to bind up any toxic molecules of Theobromine (the caffeine-like toxin in chocolate that is bad for dogs and good for women) that might still be floating around in her system. The good news was that by morning Abby looked completely normal. Folks may have wondered, though, why I was rushing out the door with the pastor's wife.

is an example of healthful people food that you may never have considered feeding your dog. Remember, when trying any new food, start with only a small amount to see if your dog can tolerate that type of food.

In a nutshell, I believe many dogs often suffer from temporary and chronic ailments due to food-related reactions. They're either getting an allergenic ingredient they shouldn't have or they're *not* getting enough of ones that they require. There's no question in my mind that commercial dog food precipitates countless canine maladies.

Chapter Four

Putting Nutrition to Work
for Your Dog

I've written a lot about the pros and cons of the various ingredients commonly found in dog food; we've even analyzed several ingredients lists from commercial foods. Now it's time that you become comfortable pulling it all together. I want you to start by thinking about all the ingredients in everything your dog eats, which will begin to help you identify and good and the bad in your dog's diet. And while you do that, we'll do a little role playing.

Island Survival: A Breakdown of Ingredients and Their Nutrients

Imagine you and your dog are taking a cruise and the ship runs out of gas, drifts onto a reef and sinks. You and your dog swim to the shore of a nearby island only to find no human inhabitants, but plenty of fresh water, wild goats, birds, rodents, berries, mangoes, insects, reptiles and abundant ocean life. What ingredients will you feed your dog, and will they be the same exact ingredients every day? If you are a dog lover like me, you are concerned about finding enough food for both of you. At the same time, your dog may be able to help out and find some food on its own. If you get hungry enough, even insects, lizards, small mammals and berries start to look pretty good. Some days you both may eat some wild goat; the next meal may include fish, fruit, even some bugs.

The ingredients of our Deserted Island Dog Diet include: wild goat, mangoes, fish, voles, sparrow, berries and grasshopper. No additional water is added to ingredients, except for saliva, stomach and intestinal juice. No grains, artificial preservatives, stabilizers or artificial flavor are added either, and the ingredients may change depending on availability...and their ability to get away.

Ingredients in diets are always listed in the order of their percentage in the food, so the first ingredient listed in our Deserted Island Dog Diet is wild goat. It makes up the majority of the diet because once you get one, it takes a few days to finish it; it's followed in descending order by the other ingredients until you get to the smallest ingredient, the one fat grasshopper that couldn't escape.

After two months you are rescued and you find out your fiancée has taken up with another and is living somewhere in Belgravia. (I was one of those people who really liked the movie *Castaway*.) In addition, both you and your dog are the picture of good health. How could that be?

The natural diet that you and your dog were forced to adopt must have contained ingredients in the right proportions. Water, proteins, carbohydrates, fats and natural preservatives contained in the native plants and animals kept you both healthy until you were rescued. The fact that the diet included voles, sparrows and a grasshopper should not worry you. Commercial dog food, too, is made up of ingredients that will never make it onto our human table, but this should not be a cause for concern. It also does not mean that the meat, vegetables, fats, oils and grains in dog food are rejects; they just do not meet current guidelines for human-grade ingredients. Meat by-products, for example, can be processed meat items that you and I would not normally eat...such as chicken gizzards, beaks and feet. This does not mean that by-products are not nutritious. Wild animals certainly eat their share of beaks and feet, but those ingredients are a small part of the whole package that contains skin, fat, organs, meat, cartilage and blood.

Now let's dig a little deeper and create a nutrient profile for the Deserted Island Dog Diet. Nutrients are the body's building blocks — the sources of energy that all living things derive from food. A list of nutrients includes carbohydrates, fats, proteins (or their building blocks, amino acids), vitamins and minerals (sodium, chloride, magnesium, calcium, phosphorous, potassium). Water and oxygen are also considered nutrients because they are essential for life. A nutrient profile is a list of the percentages of nutrients in a particular food. Now, let's have some fun with this and our Deserted Island Dog Diet. We'll combine the available ingredients found on our island and analyze this hypothetical diet for nutrients. What can we learn?

List of Ingredients — Day One of the Deserted Island Dog Diet:	
Wild Goat Mangoes Grasshopper Sea Grapes Coconuts	
Nutrient Profile of Ingredients (combined):	
Water	60%*
Protein	35
Carbohydrate	20
Fat	30
Fiber	15
Vitamins and Minerals	Adequate

*All numbers are percentages. Protein, carbohydrate, fat and fiber equal 100%; water is factored separately. The numbers are approximate values for demonstration purposes.

Water. Are you surprised to see the high percentage of water? Our bodies contain about 60 percent water; our dogs are 60 percent water. Most of the animals, plants, fruit and vegetables that our dogs (and we) eat contain at least 60 percent water. It seems logical to me then that a diet with a lot more than 10 percent water (the water content in the average dry dog food) would work better for creatures that have evolved for millions of years on a moisture-laden regimen. Water is the most important nutrient on the list. You can live for weeks without eating, but you'll perish in about a week without water.

> *It seems logical to me then that a diet with more than 10 percent water (the water content in the average dry dog food) would work better for creatures that have evolved for millions of years on a moisture-laden regimen.*

Our bodies can store excess carbohydrates and fats for fuel if food is not available, but we can store only enough water for a few days. To understand why water is so essential, you only have to think of the trillions of cells that make up our body as creatures in our own private ocean. Each of these cells needs delivery service. Water is the vehicle for deliveries in our body. Water is like our body's Universal Particle Delivery Service. Adequate water keeps the blood pressure high enough to float our red blood cells and white blood cells through our vessels, deliver fuel and take away the trash, and to be squirted out along with various enzymes to help digest our food. Without the elixir of life—water—the body will not function for long.

Proteins. Protein molecules run the show. Without them, we would be a glob of watery, sticky fat with bones bulging out. Proteins carry nutrients through the blood to the trillions of cells in our body, and even escort these nutrients through passageways and to specific workshops inside the cell. Proteins are made up of amino acids, which is important because to stay healthy the protein we eat must contain the essential amino acids that our liver cannot manufacturer. These amino acids are joined together in our cells to make up the various tissues and working proteins in our body. Picture protein molecules as a Lego model with amino acids as the small Lego pieces making up that model. Meats, eggs, nuts and beans are all excellent sources of proteins and essential amino acids. Interestingly, natural selection favors organisms that do not waste energy, so we only make amino acids that are not readily available in our food.

Amino Acids. Of the 20 standard amino acids, we need at least eight from our diet; our liver can make the other 10 to 12. Babies need a couple more than adults, and some amino acids are used to make the others. All totaled, animals need 22 amino acids, 12 of which their bodies can synthesize. The essential amino acids are arginine, histidine, isoleucine, leucine, lysine, methionine, phenylalanine, threonine, tryptophan and valine...and in cats, taurine. Dogs can synthesize the amino acid taurine, and therefore, it is not supplemented in their food. This is why dogs can eat cat food but cats will develop taurine deficiency eating dog food.

Fats. Fats are often considered to be a necessary evil of food. This important nutrient, however, together with protein makes up the cellular structure of our body. Picture our amino-acid Lego protein pieces in a circle. Alternate flexible fat pieces with protein pieces. That gives you a rough idea of the composition of the lining of your trillions of cells. The fat pieces between the protein pieces give the structure flexibility. Fat gets the bad rap because food in excess of our needs is stored as fat. But fat actually accomplishes much that is good in the body. Fat is a reserve of energy we can use—whether we're marooned on an island with our dog and need the energy to survive until the next meal or running a marathon. Fat insulates us from the cold and protects our bodies from jarring traumas that might cause damage to our internal organs. In fact, the kidneys are located pretty close to the surface—below our ribs, by our spine—and they have a nice protective layer of fat wrapped around them. We need the right amount of fat (especially Omega 3) to stay healthy.

But getting back to dog nutrition: Fats, essential fatty acids and oils are the most important supplements that you can add to make your dog's diet a healthier one. They are also the most economical and easiest to include. A healthful mix of fat contains unsaturated, monounsaturated and saturated fats. Our diets and those of our dogs do not contain enough of the first two. An animal deprived of those fatty acids will exhibit a lot of the same skin problems I see in my clinic. When those essential fats and oils are added back into the daily diet, most skin becomes healthier after a month or two.

Carbohydrates. Carbohydrates are the energy source of the body. Our blood sugar (blood glucose) is regulated to remain at a certain level to keep our trillions of cells happy and bathed in glucose. Carbohydrates not used for fuel immediately are stored in the muscles and liver as a starch called glycogen. Glycogen is a great fuel that can be easily accessed if you or your dog needs a burst of energy for play or to get away quickly. It's like stored energy. But dogs (and humans) only need just so much carbohydrate in the diet. Excess carbohydrate not used for fuel or stored as glycogen is changed into fat, which is easier and more compact to store. This is why the high level of carbohydrates in kibble makes some dogs obese.

Minerals and Vitamins. The last nutrients on a typical nutrient profile list are the minerals and vitamins. You will recognize the names of minerals such as calcium, phosphorous, potassium, iron, sodium, chloride and magnesium that make up our bones, provide the charge in our body's electrical system, help carry oxygen, and help muscles to contract and relax. Vitamins are known by the letters A, B, C, D, E and K and actually were classified with letters before their exact structure was understood. Vitamin C was known to prevent scurvy before it was named ascorbic acid.

Even though you know the names or letters, you might not know what the various vitamins do. Vitamins are molecules that the body cannot make from other nutrients but needs in order to manufacture or regulate the manufacturing of important body components. Vitamins function as hormones (Vitamin D), antioxidants (Vitamin E) and regulators of growth (Vitamin A). The largest group of vitamins (B-complex) helps molecules react together to produce other compounds. Vitamin A, by the way, is needed for the manufacture of a protein called rhodopsin that is necessary for vision in low light. It's this that is the source for the old wives' tale about carrots helping you see at night.

Just yesterday a client brought her dog in for a vaccination appointment. I noticed that the fur looked shiny, and skin that used to be red and flaky was now signficantly improved. When I glanced at the chart, I saw that this dog had visited once every month or two for skin problems in the past, and it had been a year since the last visit. "How's the skin doing?" I asked. The client mentioned that the skin really improved when she started feeding carrots every day. Carrots are on the list of healthful human foods we can feed dogs, and they are a great source of Vitamin A. It may be that more Vitamin A may be needed in the diet of dogs with skin problems.

How Many Calories Does Your Dog Need?

Before getting into this subject, I just want to say that if you eliminate dry food and treats you won't need to count calories. If you can't do that and your dog is overweight, it may help if you feed fewer calories

Let's Not Forget About Our Cats

When I graduated from veterinary school in 1980, it was not unusual to see at least two to three cats per week with urinary problems due to inflammation of the bladder or urethra from crystals that form in the concentrated urine…just like a kid's crystal rock garden. These crystals and stones that form as the rock garden grows can block the urethra and cause a life-threatening situation. If they do not block the urethra, inflammation, crystals and stones in the bladder and kidneys may lead to chronic, debilitating urinary tract and kidney infections. FUS or feline urologic syndrome, we are taught, occurs because excess calcium and phosphorous from the diet cause crystals and stones to form in the concentrated urine. To combat this problem, low-ash and acidified foods were born and have helped decrease the numbers of cats affected.

Urinary diets that change the acidity of the urine sometimes help dissolve the crystals in the urine and prevent the formation of new ones. Recent research, however, now shows that while acidified, low-ash urinary diets have resulted in fewer of one kind of crystal, they've increased the incidence of another. Have we solved the problem, with a low-ash, acidified, dry-food diet or have we just patched it? Is there a more urological solution? I wonder.

Cats are obligate carnivores. In mild climates, wild cats can survive on prey only, without drinking any water. Their prey contain a high moisture content and fewer stone-causing elements (e.g., phosphorous, calcium and oxalates). I believe that the mix of nutrients in small mammals and birds is probably the correct formula for the diets of cats. As I have pointed out in wolves, the correct mixture of ingredients may be present in the wild or natural diet. Therefore, canned foods with more moisture and less ash make a much better choice than dry food for cats with weight, diabetes and urinary problems. There seems to be an epidemic of obesity, inflammatory bowel disease (chronic vomiting and diarrhea), diabetes and dry skin in cats eating dry food. Sound familiar? I'm thinking that this calls for another book…one about cat nutrition. How about *More Mice Than Rice: Sensible Nutrition for Your Domesticated Predator*?

Common health problems such as obesity, diabetes, inflammatory bowel disease and urinary-tract problems found in our domesticated dogs and cats—both of them eating diets with similar ingredients—have caused me to reevaluate the types of diets we feed each species.

and encourage exercise. But how few calories and how much more exercise? Is a dog calorie the same as a human calorie? How many calories does a Chihuahua need versus a Great Dane, or a working dog versus a couch dweller? Judging by questions I've seen posted on the Internet and from my clients, this is an area that bears discussion.

Each type of diet or treat contains a certain number of calories per ounce. Calories are beginning to be included on the labels of dog food, but you need to know how to apply the information. If the calories are not listed, you can go to the particular brand's website and usually find what you need. Somewhere, it will probably tell you the number of calories your dog's food contains per ounce, per cup, per pound or per kilogram. So now, all you have to do is figure out how many ounces you need to feed per day for your dog's size, activity level, and metabolic rate (how readily they burn calories), and then you will know how much food to put in the bowl once or twice daily. Sound easy?

Don't worry, I'm not suggesting you dust off your old geometry or calculus textbook to figure out the formula, but there are a few things you need to know. Let's start with kibble and dry treats. They have shapes and densities that you have to consider. If you took a measuring cup and poured out 8 ounces of kibble and weighed it, the scale would show that the amount of food only weighed 3 ounces to 4 ounces (minus the cup). If each 8-ounce cup of kibble actually contains roughly 3 ounces to 4 ounces of food, and you found on the website that your dog's kibble contains about 100 calories per ounce, then you know that each 8-ounce cup of kibble contains between 300 calories and 400 calories. That is the difference between weight in ounces by density on a scale and by volume using a measuring cup.

Before we go on, let's be honest. This example of an 8-ounce measuring cup is not reality. Most people use a 2-cup scoop or measuring

 ## Kilograms to Ounces—A Quick Conversion

Another horrifying math conversion found on many websites has to do with calories expressed as calories per kilogram. As Americans, we need to know the number of calories per ounce in order to easily calculate the daily calories consumed. You can change calories per kilogram to calories per pound by multiplying by 0.453 (or, for simplicity, by one half). So, if the food label states that there are 3600 kilocalories per kilogram (remember kilocalories and calories are the same term), we can divide 3600 in half to come up with approximately 1800 calories per pound. As there are 16 ounces in a pound, we can further divide 1800 by 16 to get roughly 110 calories per ounce. If you're a stickler for accuracy, multiply 3600 by 0.453 and divide by 16; you'll get exactly 101.92 calories per ounce. If each cup holds 3 to 4 ounces of kibble, then each 8-ounce cup delivers between 300 and 400 calories to your dog.

cup, a large plastic cup or bowl, or they just dig in with their hand and toss the food in the bowl. Yet another potentially confusing thing I noticed on the websites is that the terms *kilocalories* and *calories* are used interchangeably. Just so we're clear, they both refer to the same thing: The amount of energy contained in a certain food. The original definition for the calorie is based on the metric system. One food calorie (1 kcal or 1,000 calories) is the amount of digestively available food energy (by burning it) required to raise the temperature of one quart of water about 2 degrees Fahrenheit. That is the same for humans, dogs, cats and any other living thing that comes to mind. One Science Diet chicken-and-rice, medium-size treat contains 20 calories, which could raise the temperature 40 degrees when burned up. This explanation does not really help you with how much to feed your dog, but I figured if I had to suffer through four years of chemistry, a paragraph here and there wouldn't hurt you any.

I hope my rambling, quasi-math, rounded-off example helps you make your necessary conversions. After hours of searching,

I found a website with a chart that lists 125 brands of dry dog food and the calories contained in a cup of each of them. I started to add them all together and was going to divide the answer by 125 to get an average, but I quickly saw that the numbers really didn't differ drastically among brands. I glanced over the chart several times and estimated the average of most dry food to be in the 45 calories per ounce range or an average of 360 calories per cup or 90 calories per ounce by weight (remember each cup of dry food contains 3 ounces to 4 ounces of ingredients. So 360 calories divided by 4 is 90 calories per ounce).

With canned food, calories are a bit easier to calculate. Eight ounces of canned food in a measuring cup weighs about 8 ounces, so calories can be easily calculated by knowing the calories per ounce — most come in around 35 calories to 40 calories per ounce. Different brands of commercial canned food come in different sizes of cans, so you have to know how many ounces your particular can of dog food contains to calculate the calories per can. To compare with dry food, an average cup of canned food at 35 calories per ounce contains 285 calories, which amounts to 75 fewer calories per cup.

Well that's half the battle. Armed with data about the calories per ounce in the bag or can you are serving your dog, you now need to know how many ounces of the food you should feed your dog. This depends on your dog's weight and activity level. It's difficult to find a simple chart that gives you the amount of calories your dog needs per pound because some dogs burn more calories than others. Some burn off energy just by looking at you and quivering. According to some charts, dogs need between 10 calories and 50 calories per pound. You can see that the range is quite broad. Common sense says that growing puppies, nursing mothers, athletes and working dogs need more calories than most canine couch potatoes. Small dogs tend to have a higher metabolism and usually burn more calories per pound than big dogs.

Employing the 10-calorie-to-50-calorie-per-pound range, big dogs, obese dogs and couch potatoes need about 10 calories per pound. Using that figure, you should feed a 30-pound, weight-challenged couch potato about 300 calories per day, which translates to 8 ounces of kibble (3 ounces to 4 ounces by weight) or slightly more than half of the 13-ounce can of dog food in front of me. The label (yes this one actually lists the number of calories) states there are 504 Kcals/calories in the whole can. Tucker, my 90-pound Lab, thrives on this formula twice a day and looks great. (90 pounds x 10 calories per pound couch potato activity = 900 calories per day.)

Referring again to the charts, my little 10-pound dog Maisy (small and more active than Tucker) needs to eat between 20 and 30 calories per pound. In fact, Maisy eats about 300 calories per day and is doing just fine. *The take-home lessons from all of this are pretty simple:*

1. Know that a cup of dry food by volume is equal to slightly less than half a cup of dry food by weight.
2. Don't let the kilo in kilocalories confuse you. If your dog looks and feels good on the amount you are feeding, you should have no worries.
3. If your dog is too heavy, reduce his portion of dry food; dilute it with broth, water or green beans; or take him off of kibble and feed him a less calorie-dense canned food.

Here's a little chart to help you. I've used a 10-pound dog for all examples; you can apply this guide to all dogs. The key is to select a calories-per-pound option and multiply by the weight of your dog. Remember, that smaller dogs usually need more calories per pound than a large dog; active dogs also need more calories per pound. Your dog may require less or more food due to its metabolic rate.

Dog Weight	Obese/ Activity	Calories per pound	Calories per day	Amount by oz. kibble volume per day/13 oz. can
10	Obese	8	80	1 ¾ oz./ ¼ can
10	Lazy	10	100	2 oz./ ⅓ can
10	Walks every-where	20	200	5 oz./ ½ can
10	Runs around a lot	30	300	6 oz./ ¾ can
10	Hyper/ neurotic/ crazed	40–50	400–500	8–10 oz./ 1 can

*This chart is only meant to give you an idea of how to use your pet's weight and temperament to correctly gauge the amount of dry or canned food to feed **per day**. To be accurate, you have to also include calories from the healthful human foods you use as treats as well as any other treats such as biscuits or chews. The Science Diet chicken-and-rice package does not list the calories, but on the website I found that each biscuit contains 20 calories. The package states that I can feed a dog of Tucker's weight 10 biscuits daily (200 calories or 25% of his daily diet). In practice, Tucker gets 3 or 4 daily as part of the "nummy nite-time" treat ritual. If your pet has problems, consider the calories, the ingredients and different types of treats.*

Nature, Nutrients and Diets: A Comparative Nutritional Chart

I don't know about you, but I find charts helpful. They synthesize a lot of information into a form that often brings great clarity. So I think it's about time I give you a nutritional chart that makes it easy to compare nutrient profiles in different types of food. I've arranged the chart to include the most popular types of commercially prepared diets so we can see how they compare with the natural diet of the

wolf. The list of key nutrients (water, protein, carbohydrate and
is in the column on the far left. The percentages of each nutrient in
the diets are in the body of the table.

	Dry food or treats	Canned diet	Homemade chicken & rice	Raw diet	Wolf diet
Water	10%*	75	70	70	70
Protein	20	30	35	35	50
Carbo-hydrates	65	40	35	35	<10
Fat	10	20	20	20	35

*All numbers are percentages. They are averages and do not add up to 100%.

A couple of points about the chart I should clarify:

- Because I listed only the averages for protein, carbohydrate and
  fat nutrients in the diets and did not include fiber or ash, the
  percentages will not add up to exactly 100 percent.
- Water is measured separately. In the case of the wolf diet, 70
  percent is water; of the remaining 30 percent, 50 percent is protein, <10 percent is carbohydrate and 35 percent is fat. The rest
  are fiber, ash, vitamin and mineral nutrients.
- The commercial food averages are based on the ingredients in
  products I feed my animals and sell in my clinic. These products are
  all sold in local pet stores and on commercial, dog food websites.
- These numbers are for comparison purposes only and do not
  include nutrient percentages from all types of dry, canned or
  raw diets (nor are they representative of all commercial foods
  available or all wolf diets).
- I included the wolf diet to give us something to compare against.
  The nutrient-percentages data are based on Dr. David Mech's
  research. The percentages of nutrients that wolves eat will vary
  by geographic area and time of year.

The nutrient averages in the chart point out obvious differences between most commercial diets and the wolf diet. The most dramatic difference is the percentage of water: Dry diets contain only about 10 percent water, compared with 70 percent to 80 percent water in the canned, raw and wolf diets. The 10-percent moisture content of dry food and treats render them about as moist as an ancient cookie. The canned and raw diets (80 percent and 70 percent, respectively) are about as close to nature's diet as a commercial food can get. If you believe like I do that our dogs' digestive systems have evolved across the millennia to process moister diets, then the moist diet is more likely the healthier choice. I think that moister diets (canned or raw) and diluted dry food are easier to digest, less irritating to the bowel and less stressful for the kidneys to process.

Also significant are the differences in the carbohydrate category. Dry food and treats contain many more carbohydrates than any other type of diet. Wolves are omnivores but with a heavy slant toward being carnivores since they eat a lot of meat when times are good. Compared to their ancestors, the domestic dog is being fed any where from two to six times more carbohydrates. This is undoubtedly profitable for manufacturers, but I don't think it's healthy for all dogs. This is particularly true since the most commonly used carbohydrates in commercial dog food are grains such as wheat (in about 50 percent of the diets and 80 percent of the treats) or corn.

Don't get me wrong. As I've explained before, carbohydrates play an important role. As glucose, carbohydrates are the fuel for the trillions of cells in our bodies...and those of our dogs. Glucose needs to be at a certain level in the blood, and if that level drops too low, you (or your dog) will pass out. If that glucose level is not corrected, you (or your dog) will die. Now I have your attention! That does not mean, however, that more is better. The liver and muscles store a certain

Dr. Greg's Good Ingredients List

As you know by now, I like to give my dogs a variety of healthful ingredients. It's good for them, and they like the change. Whether you decide to use these ingredients as food toppers, treats or the basis for making your own dog food, you need to know the calories so you don't overfeed. In sensible quantities, healthful people food will not make your dog fat, but you do have to factor the calories into the full day's allotment. This chart will help you get an idea of the calories contained in healthful human ingredients that you may want to include in your dog's daily diet.

Ingredients	Calories	Ingredients	Calories
Proteins		**Veggies (good carbs)**	
Chicken frozen or cooked, 1 thigh	200	Green beans, 2 oz.	20
Chicken lunchmeat, 1 slice	60	Carrots, 2 oz.	15
Chicken hotdog, 1.6 oz.	120	Squash, 2 oz.	10
Turkey lunchmeat, 1 slice	60		
Turkey hotdog, 1.6 oz.	100	**Other Carbs**	
Pork loin/chop, 2 oz.	150	Potato, medium	60
Ham lunchmeat, 1 slice	50	Rice, 2 oz.	50
Bacon, 3 pieces	100		
Salmon, 2 oz.	120	**Fats/Oils**	
Tilapia, 2 oz.	60	Olive/Canola, 1 Tblsp	120
Tuna, 2 oz.	60	Olive/Canola, 1 tsp	40
Shrimp, 2 oz.	60	Fish-oil, 1 capsule	10
Egg, 1 yolk	80	Chicken skin, from breast or thigh	50
Cheese cheddar/ swiss, 2 oz.	200	Bacon fat, 1 tsp	30

amount of excess carbohydrates as glycogen that is stored energy. Carbohydrates also form the structural components in plants, and in animals are important for our immune, reproductive and blood-clotting systems. Beyond that, any extra carbohydrate is turned into fat. That leaves me concerned about the choice of ingredient (wheat and corn versus rice, potato and vegetables) and the amount (60 percent of the dry diet versus 10 percent of the wolf's diet).

Now that I've piqued your interest in carbohydrates, I have to warn you that many dog food manufacturers do not list carbs on their nutrient analysis labels. It's time for us to get out our calculators again, but don't worry. The math is easy. If a nutrient label lists protein 25 percent, fat 10 percent, fiber 5 percent and ash 5 percent, then the carbohydrate content is calculated as 55 percent: 100% total nutrients minus 45% (protein, fat, fiber and ash) = 55%.

The Good Doctor's Sage Advice: Making My Case for Fats and Oils

If you and your dog should come to my clinic for a consultation, I would first examine the condition of your dog's skin and hair coat. I'd check its weight and ask you about any known allergies or medical conditions. Because some dogs fare better on some types of diets or different ingredients than others, I would apply simple nutritional truths, as I've laid them out in these pages, in order to discover what diet is best for your dog.

If your dog has dry, flaky skin, you (and your dog) are not alone. The fact is that 50 percent of all dogs have dry skin. The good news is that this condition is easy to treat—when you know how. I'd recommend adding extra oils and fats to the diet. You would think that if commercial dry diets were nutritionally "complete and balanced" for all dogs (as advertised) there would be little to no improvement in the skin and coat after we added fats and oils to the diet. In fact, if you add oils daily or at least several times a week, you should see a difference in two to three months—the coat will look shiny and the flakes will disappear.

The best way to incorporate fats and oils into the diet is to add a healthful mixture of oils, such as olive oil, canola oil, fish-oil capsules and/or egg yolks directly to the dry or wet food. I used olive oil as a supplement until Lonna brought home a bottle for our own consumption that contained a healthful mixture of olive, canola and flax oils. I had noticed that Archie was more reluctant to eat his food since I'd started mixing olive oil in it, so I poured a tablespoon of the new oil mixture on his food. He loved this new blend, and Lonna had to get another bottle for us.

I add 1 teaspoon to 1 tablespoon of oil per dog daily, depending on the dog's size and medical issues. This amounts to about a teaspoon for small dogs and a tablespoon for large dogs. Dogs with dry skin, allergies and ear problems may need double that amount. I have to be truthful and tell you that I never measure all that accurately. The measurement will become a "glug" or a "drizzle" as you get more comfortable with adding the oil. To help you remember to add the oil, leave the bottle in plain sight for a few weeks—but not in direct sun or in a hot place as oils easily become rancid. Rancid oils are worse than no oil at all.

Egg yolks are a great source of protein and fat, and many home-made dog diets recommend including them. If raw eggs make you nervous because of the low risk of *Salmonella* infection, cook them.

Lonna was leery about adding raw eggs and made me consume a raw-egg drink for a week to make sure her precious pets would not get sick. I reminded her that wolves eat rotten carcasses and that our dogs often eat poop, garbage and dead things they find along the road. This statement earned me an, "I really didn't want that much information" glare.

The veterinary profession and commercial, dog food companies also warn against feeding raw eggs and other raw foods. Elderly people, infants and those with a compromised immune system are the most at risk for life-threatening infections from a *Salmonella*-contaminated egg or *E. coli* hamburger. The rest of the population may only experience flu-like symptoms. In my opinion, the chances are greater that your dog will have poor health or allergies due to the commercial dog food or treats that it eats than that it will become ill due to *Salmonella* or *E. coli*.

The ultimate decision is one you'll have to make after you do the research and weigh the risks and benefits. I mix an egg yolk in my dogs' food two to three times a week. Archie was reluctant to eat his food when I mixed a whole, raw egg in his bowl; he preferred just the yolk. Some of my clients also have reported that their dogs don't like egg whites. Some dogs may balk when the whole egg is mixed in, or they'll vomit or have indigestion. By the way, did you know you can use human Pepcid to treat a dog for an upset stomach? I give 1/2 a pill to small dogs and a whole pill to medium and large dogs.

Fish-oil capsules have become a morning treat at the Martinez house. When I open the cupboard and grab the bottle of fish-oil capsules, the dogs hear the rattle and come to get their morning pill. I have to admit they don't like them as much as Lonna's chicken-and-rice treats or the other healthful goodies we give them, but they have acquired a taste for them. When we take our pills together, it helps to remind me to take my own. I've been taking two daily and counseling clients to give one to three pills each day for each dog. Small dogs get one capsule, medium dogs get two and large dogs get three capsules, once a day. Dogs with severe allergy problems may need one capsule extra. Fish oil helps keep the skin, immune system, heart and joints healthy as well. It seems the only thing it doesn't help are the fish.

One of my patients became very nauseous after eating a fish-oil capsule and needs to get its fat-nutrient requirements from other sources, such as canola oil, flax seed oil or fish treats (e.g., salmon, tuna fish, tilapia scraps). Remember, all dogs are individuals and have different tolerances for different ingredients. After a few months, my dog Maisy did not come running for her "fish pill" and acted nauseous a few mornings after that. She's prone to nausea if she eats common allergenic food or treats and will go out and eat grass and throw up. A half of a Pepcid and she feels much better. After a few years, her system clearly did not tolerate fish-oil capsules. Any dog can develop allergies from eating food that they have enjoyed symptom-free for years.

My dogs love chicken skins, salmon skins, pork, ham, even bacon fat in small amounts. Although they would eat larger amounts if they could, I use caution, and so should you. Feeding fat to a dog with pancreatitis may be life threatening. Be very cautious when offering any amount of fat to your pet. And particularly, do not feed beef scraps or beef fat to any pet suffering from medical problems such as pancreatitis, or to any dog prone to intestinal allergies, diarrhea, vomiting or who clears the room with gas.

> " *Test your dog's tolerance to any new diet, meat, treat or fat. Start with very small portions.* "

Test your dog's tolerance to any new diet, meat, treat or fat. Start with very small portions. In my experience, beef, beef fat, corn and wheat gluten are the most common causes of medical problems and food reactions. Of course, not all dogs are intolerant of beef, wheat and corn, but those that have symptoms of allergies should avoid them. Other ingredients and diets can cause similar reactions in some dogs. Rottweilers always break the rules. Robin, our veterinary technician, has a Rottweiler that is very sensitive to chicken products but can eat beef just fine. That's why you should feed a small amount of the new food for two or three days to see how your dog reacts before feeding a normal daily amount.

10 Rules for Your Dog's Better Health

1. *Know what ingredients are in your dog's food, treats and chews.* Read the ingredient label on the back; do not rely on the label or pictures on the front of the bag, can or box to show you what's inside.

2. *If your dog is suffering from skin, ear, seizures, stomach or bowel problems, a hypoallergenic diet with added healthful fats and oils may help.* If your vet has ruled out other medical conditions, pick a diet that does not contain beef, meat by-products, meat digest, beef liver, wheat, wheat gluten, corn or corn gluten. Remember, it's also possible that your dog is allergic to other meats or grains. A case in point is Robin's Rottweiler that is allergic to chicken. Then too, our vegetarian-escape artist canine, Susie La Faille, did well on a no-meat diet. Always test a small portion of any trial food or treat for a few days to avoid uncomfortable flare-ups.

3. *Consider canned dog food.* Kibble is the most popular and convenient dog food on the market today. But if your dog is obese or has moderate-

to-severe skin, ear, stomach or bowel problems, canned food may be a better choice. Canned food generally has about a third fewer calories per serving than kibble (remember you can further dilute the calories in kibble with water, broth or veggies). And canned food may be easier on the stomach and bowel as long as the ingredients are not allergenic to your dog. It's a common myth that the poop will be runny because the food is. If that were the case, we could never eat soup. Should diarrhea occur, it's probably because the canned food contains allergenic ingredients such as beef, wheat or corn, not because of more moisture. It's critical to know the ingredients in order to avoid medical problems such as itching, vomiting, seizures and diarrhea.

4. **Dogs that react adversely to every type of dog food and many different ingredients may be reacting to the preservatives, stabilizers or other additives in the food.** The sensitive bowel of these troubled dogs may not be able to handle all the different non-food chemicals that find their way into most commercial foods. The symptoms of these poor, miserable creatures may improve when we share or prepare wholesome, healthful, human foods or when they are fed hypoallergenic diets. Examples are raw diets, holistic diets and organic diets with ingredients that are not allergenic and contain few preservatives.

5. **Supplement your dog's diet with healthful fats and oils.** Fat has a bad rap because some dogs cannot tolerate beef fat and because of non-medical references in the media made about unhealthful fat. There is mounting evidence, however, that healthful fats and oils are critical for good health. When I add olive oil, canola oil and fish-oil capsules to the diet, dogs with dry skin and other skin problems usually improve. Egg yolk is a great way to increase the fats and protein quality in one fell swoop. I add one raw egg yolk with a bit of the white attached three times a week. My dogs do not like much egg white; your dogs may be different.

6. **Treats are the crack cocaine of the canine world.** Dogs crave them at the expense of their health. If you must feed store-bought,

biscuit-like treats, at least find healthful ones that do not contain beef and wheat. Better still, feed healthful treats such as poultry, fish, pork, carrots or green beans. And never offer your dog chocolate or chewing gum. One pet-health website lists grapes, raisins, onions, garlic, macadamia nuts, avocado, raw eggs and wild mushrooms as dangerous. These are mildly toxic foods, and an especially sensitive dog may become sick, as might a dog that ingests large quantities or eats them for a long period of time. In my experience, however, spoiled food in the garbage, snail bait, rat poison, chocolate, antifreeze and now chewing gum cause 99 percent of reported poisonings. I have never seen an animal presented for any food toxicity except spoiled food, chocolate, moldy walnuts, wild mushrooms and, of course, high-carbohydrate, allergenic, low-fat commercial dog food.

7. *Chewing bones for short periods of time can help clean the teeth and keep the gums healthy.* The time most dogs spend chewing dental health biscuits is much shorter than the time it took me to type this sentence. Most dogs practically inhale a biscuit or treat, which does nothing for their teeth and gums. The decision to let your dogs chew on bones should not be taken lightly. Dogs that tend to grab and swallow are not good candidates for chewing. If dental tartar is not a problem, they may not need to chew anyway. Every two weeks, I give my dogs raw knucklebones, smoked pork bones, frozen or raw chicken thighs or pigs' ears as dental chew treats. I avoid rawhide chew products because they seem to cause the most medical problems of any treats. Rawhide is beef skin, and dogs allergic to beef meat will also be allergic to beef skin. I recommend avoiding rawhide if your dog has any skin, ear, seizure, stomach or bowel problems. I suspect rawhide can cause seizures in sensitive individuals anytime from a few hours to 48 hours after being eaten.

8. *Don't underestimate the value of variety in the diet.* If you think eating the same type of baked, highly preserved, high-carbohydrate, dry, hard kibble daily for years would be good for your

health or if your dog is thriving on dry food, then there may be no reason to change the diet. However, if your dog is overweight or if you notice any nausea, diarrhea, dry skin, occasional itchiness or inflamed skin or ears, a change in the ingredients (and especially the addition of fats, oils, eggs and healthful human food) may be beneficial.

9. *Special diets with medical-sounding names may be no better than any other commercial diet.* How a particular type of dog food and its ingredients affect your pet is more important than the name. Life-stage diets and breed-specific diets vary in the type and quality of ingredients. My older dogs have always been fed high-quality, chicken-and-vegetable canned food (also duck-and-potato canned food). That is their life-stage diet. Breed-specific diets contain hypoallergenic ingredients because purebred dogs often suffer more allergies than mutts. Weight-reducing diets lower the already insufficient fat levels and rarely work because of the calorie-dense, high-carbohydrate ingredients. On a low-fat diet, your obese dog may just get dryer, flakier skin. You can address the same issues with the right ingredients and a few supplements in the diet.

10. *Use caution and common sense.* Dogs with pancreatitis, diabetes, kidney and bladder problems including stone formation, liver problems, seizures and other medical conditions may benefit from changes in the diet, but these changes should be made cautiously and under the supervision of your pet's veterinarian. Changing the diet can be very stressful on a dog with moderate-to-severe medical problems. On the other hand, a dog with chronic pancreatitis may benefit from a homemade diet; a holistic, preservative-free diet; or, like my receptionist's dog Duke, the dry Hill's I/D diet. Duke did not do as well on the first two. Furthermore, I have found that it may take a month on a more healthful, hypoallergenic diet before you can lower the amount of seizure medication your dog is taking daily. The skin takes a few months to react to healthful feeding practices; it could be the same for the brain.

Using my suggestions as your guidelines, I hope that you will feel more comfortable coming up with a way to feed that fits your pet's needs, your eating habits and your pocketbook.

Living the Dream: A Great Past and a Hopeful Future

I have always wanted to be a veterinarian. From an early age, domestic and wild creatures fascinated me and led to my decision to dedicate my professional life to the happiness and health of animals. Achieving this goal and practicing veterinary medicine for almost 30 years now has been the fulfillment of that childhood dream.

Perhaps it's ironic that my education taught me to ask questions because my experiences with the therapeutic results of both nutritional and medical therapy on my pets and patients have caused me to question commercial diets and veterinary nutritional dogma. The combination of reflection upon my zoology education and my own attempts to eat a healthful diet in a world of fast food revealed to me some basic nutritional truths.

In the not too distant past, all beings ate food that was much different than 80 percent of the food sold today for either human or canine consumption. The diet evolution of canines and humans across millions of years has resulted in digestive systems finely tuned to that heredity. This is why I spend so much time comparing commercial diets with the natural diet of the dog's ancestors and wolves.

The positive results and encouraging feedback I've received when I use both nutritional and medical therapy in treating my patients and my own dogs has changed the way I view nutrition. No longer is nutrition just a chart or a list of percentages to me. It is a living mosaic of ingredients that have kept humans and their canine companions healthy for millennia.

I hope the next few years will see holistic and hypoallergenic diets mainstreamed to represent the majority instead of the minority of diets. A good example of this process is occurring with a brand of healthful dog and cat food called Spot's Stew. It all began when Andi Brown started feeding a healthier holistic diet to her cat Spot because veterinary-prescribed treatments were not helping. Spot did well, and Andi's pet food was so popular with dog and cat owners that she started producing it commercially. I've fed Spot's to my animals for at least 10 years and have counseled clients to do the same. This dog and cat food has become so popular it is now available in pet food stores and has begun competing against the "big dogs." I hope for the sake of our pets that the mix of ingredients and type of food that Spot's represents becomes the norm.

Archie, my Wire-Haired Terrier, passed away recently, but he was happy and healthy to the end. In fact, I came home for lunch one day to find him at peace on his pillow. He was 16, and getting progressively more senile and uncoordinated. I appreciate that I did not have to make the dreaded decision that Lonna and I had been discussing in the weeks preceding his passing. Even though he could not see or hear well in his last few years, when my motions and his unfailing internal clock indicated feeding time, Archie jumped, cavorted and almost tumbled with joy. I was always afraid that he'd hurt himself.

The healthier, varied diets that I feed cause all of my dogs to gather around me and do the happy dance at feeding time. Feeding them different foods has definitely made eating more interesting for them.

One morning, after I added two egg yolks, four fish-oil pills and a couple tablespoons of olive oil to a bowl containing a combination of Spot's Stew and duck-and-potato canned dog food, Lonna said, "I remember when you used to make breakfast for me!"

"If you'll act as excited and happy about breakfast as our dogs," I replied, "I'll feed you breakfast too!!"

Appendix A

I'm sure it's no surprise to you that the commercial, dog food industry is a multi-billion dollar market today. You might not know, however, that this market has been about 150 years in the making. With the permission of *Petfood Industry Magazine*, I have excerpted the following from their article entitled "The History of The Pet Food Industry." You will find more history and statistics about pet food and its manufacturing when you visit their website http://petfoodindustry.com.

What I find most interesting about the rise, growth and maturation of the pet food market is how from the very beginning manufacturers sought to serve their customers both convenience and quality while taking advantage of surplus and inexpensive meats, meat by-products, grains and other ingredients. It's a difficult balance to maintain. Furthermore, as the market for commercial foods has grown, I feel it's taken on even more of a one-size-fits-all aspect—even with the advent of many different brands, types, flavors and prescriptions.

My take-away lesson for readers is that there are many good commercial products available. The question is which ones are best for your dog. You'll need to study ingredients, observe how your dog reacts and make adjustments until you find the right diet. I always recommend:

1. Starting by eliminating the three most common allergens—beef, wheat and corn.
2. Observing your dog's health and reaction to foods. Your dog may be different.
3. Choosing wet food rather than dry because the formula more closely resembles the natural diet of wolves and the earliest ancestors of our domestic dogs.

The benefits to you will be a happy, healthy pet and, quite probably, smaller veterinarian bills. And now, enjoy these excerpts.

The History of The Pet Food Industry

The Birth of the commercial dog food business must be attributed to the inventor of the first "dog cake," a carefully compounded preparation of blended wheat meals, vegetables, beetroot and meat by James Spratt. The brilliant hunch that there was a market for proprietary dog food came to him while he was in London, in 1860…Spratt was offered some inedible, discarded ship biscuits for his dog and thereupon decided his pet was worthy of more consideration. Being of inventive mind, he devised a "dog cake" which was nutritious and inexpensive….

While it was an American who created the first dog food, it was [a] British enterprise which monopolized the market for almost 50 years, until 1907, when the F. H. Bennett Biscuits Co. was organized. Bennett's start at Avenue D and 10th St., New York City, heralded the introduction of Milk-Bone dog biscuits as the first domestic canine food…but the dog biscuit business was discouraging and the company was in the red. As a health addict with a sincere interest in nutrition, Bennett began experimenting with specialties.

One of his ideas was a bone-shaped biscuit for dogs. His aim was to produce a biscuit with nourishing ingredients to include meat, cereals, milk and food minerals fortified in liver oil, wheat germ and irradiated yeast to provide essential vitamins for dogs....

Until 1922 commercial dog food meant one of two things, either Spratt's or Milk-Bone. Shelf stocks did not move rapidly and a buyer often found the contents green with mold. Containers lacked today's standards of excellence and the fat content often turned rancid. The industry needed something to progress.

It appeared when P. M. Chappel an old time horse dealer and horse breeder with connections in the packing industry, canned dog food at Rockford, IL, under the Ken-L-Ration brand....The Chappels had trouble getting Congress to authorize transportation of this "dog food" from state to state due to the intense sentiment against use of horses.

Like all good ideas, however, the Chappels proved that dogs ate horsemeat greedily and, as the turmoil declined, the brothers tried to increase their equine meat source by raising as many as 20,000 mares...and eventually was one of the factors which caused financial tragedy in the middle 1930's.

The brothers were wise and switched horses, as they did a complete turnabout and began to produce dry dog food. Further, they recommended the mixture of dry dog with canned dog food as an ideal combination—a pioneer stroke of good merchandising still used today.

The emergence of dog biscuits, kibble and canned horsemeat as basic categories of commercial pet food paved the way for a major new dry formula called dog meal. The pioneer was Gaines Food Co., Sherburne, NY, under Clarence Gaines, who joined the concern in 1925....

The veterinarian profession turned its attention to pet food in late 1920s when Dr. Leon Whitney, D.V.M., Orange, CT, created a Bal-O-Ration brand dog food as the result of intensive research based on the conviction that dogs, like humans, need a scientifically balanced ration to reach and hold a peak of health. The brand was later sold to Tioga Mills, Waverly, NY, was succeeded by a Pampa brand which eventually was bought by Quaker Oats Co.

When Milk-Bone was acquired by National Biscuits Co. in 1931, the idea of using commercially prepared dog foods was still very much ahead of its time. Most dog foods were basically made from waste products and people were reluctant to spend money on food for their dogs. The knowledge that dogs, as well as people, had nutritional needs which must be satisfied was by no means wide spread....The missionary job was given to Nabisco's army of 3,000 salesmen who called upon the nation's food stores....

The Depression of the `30s may have meant hard times for industry, but the merchandising of dog food germinated and spread countrywide. One report accounted for 221 brands of canned dog food with about 200 of this total produced at a half dozen canning plants. The plants did the canning; the merchandisers supplied labels. The situation was similar with dry pet foods. All that was needed was a brand name and empty bags....

AAFCO [Association of American Feed Control Officials], formed in 1909, had proved to be the determining authority at the state level for the legality of copy on pet food packages. Early labels of the Great Depression Era differed little in mandatory copy from those of today. Ingredients of the `30s were meat, meat by-products, soybean meal, barley, rice, bran, green bone, vegetables, cod liver oil and charcoal....

For the year 1941, canned dog foods had represented 91% of the poundage sales and dry the remaining 9%. After the War, in 1946, canned dog food, after almost complete decimation [due largely to tin shortages during WWII], had crept up to 15%, while dry maintained domination by 85%. By 1960 canned dog food held 60% of the pet food volume while dry claimed approximately 40%....

[The 1950s...] Spratt's Patent, Ltd., chose this time to sell its American rights to General Mills, Inc., and the century-old brand faded from domestic view.

Another dimension was added to pet foods in 1957 when Ralston Purina challenged the predominant position of meal type products by introducing expanded dog food. Just pop corn tastes better than dried corn, the expanded variety offered a greater palatability by a fat coating on each particle and a chewy, crunchy texture dogs relished.

The exploded bulkiness of the new product resulted in much larger bags for the same weight as meal—a feature not overlooked at the supermarket level.....The search for untapped markets brought to light two more avenues for exploitation; namely special prescription diets and supplements known as treats or snacks. Hill's brand led the move for therapeutic distribution while Hartz sparked others to ventures into treats. Both approaches brought lasting, lucrative results....

[In the 1960s...] Throughout the country other top corporations concentrated efforts to "buy in" and share the profits as table scraps disappeared as the industry's greatest competitor....Diversification, too, became the keystone of success. Hundreds of new products tested the creative ingenuity of advertising agencies, research divisions, and sales executives. Just as the biggest food chains realized the battle was no longer with Mom and Pop outlets—but rather among themselves—so did the predominant dozen pet food manufacturers learn that growth, for them, was to come from penetrating markets of their biggest competitors.

Appendix B

Interpreting Pet Food Labels *by David A. Dzanis, DVM, Ph.D., DACVN*

The following excerpt can be found in its entirety on the US Department of Health & Human Services (US Food and Drug Administration) wesite. You can find this article by following this link: http://www.fda.gov/AnimalVeterinary/ResourcesforYou/UCM047113.

The product name is the first part of the label noticed by the consumer, and can be a key factor in the consumer's decision to buy the product. For that reason, manufacturers often use fanciful names or other techniques to emphasize a particular aspect. Since many consumers purchase a product based on the presence of a specific ingredient, many product names incorporate the name of an ingredient to highlight its inclusion in the product. The percentages of named ingredients in the total product are dictated by four AAFCO rules.

The "95%" rule applies to products consisting primarily of meat, poultry or fish, such as some of the canned products. They have simple names, such as "Beef for Dogs" or "Tuna Cat Food." In these examples, at least 95% of the product must be the named ingredient (beef or tuna, respectively), not counting the water added for processing and "condiments." Counting the added water, the named ingredient still must comprise 70% of the product. Since ingredient lists must be declared in the proper order of predominance by weight, "beef" or "tuna" should be the first ingredient listed, followed often by water, and then other components such as vitamins and minerals. If the name includes a combination of ingredients, such as "Chicken 'n Liver Dog Food," the two together must comprise 95% of the total weight. The first ingredient named in the product name must be the one of higher predominance in the product. For example, the product could not be named "Lobster and Salmon for Cats" if there is more salmon than lobster in the product. Because this rule only applies to ingredients of animal origin, ingredients that are not from a meat, poultry or fish source, such as grains and vegetables, cannot be used as a component of the 95% total. For example, a "Lamb and Rice Dog Food" would be misnamed unless the product was comprised of at least 95% lamb.

The "25%" or "dinner" rule applies to many canned and dry products. If the named ingredients comprise at least 25% of the product (not counting the water for processing), but less than 95%, the name must include a qualifying descriptive term, such as "Beef Dinner for Dogs." Many descriptors other than "dinner" are used, however. "Platter," "entree," "nuggets" and "formula" are just a few examples. Because, in this example, only one-quarter of the product must be beef, it would most likely be found third or fourth on the ingredient list. Since the primary ingredient is not always the named ingredient, and may in fact be an ingredient that is not desired, the ingredient list should always be checked before purchase. For example, a cat owner may have learned from his or her finicky feline to avoid buying products with fish in it, since the cat doesn't like fish. However, a "Chicken Formula Cat Food" may not always be the best choice, since some "chicken formulas" may indeed contain fish, and sometimes may contain even more fish than chicken. A quick check of the ingredient list would avert this mistake.

If more than one ingredient is included in a "dinner" name, they must total 25% and be listed in the same order as found on the ingredient list. Each named ingredient must be at least 3% of the total, too. Therefore, "Chicken n' Fish Dinner Cat Food" must have 25% chicken and fish combined, and at least 3% fish. Also, unlike the "95%" rule, this rule applies to all ingredients, whether of animal origin or not. For example, a "Lamb and Rice Formula for Cats" would be an acceptable name as long as the amounts of lamb and rice combined totaled 25%.

The "3%" or "with" rule was originally intended to apply only to ingredients highlighted on the principal display panel, but outside the product name, in order to allow manufacturers to point out the presence of minor ingredients that were not added in sufficient quantity to merit a "dinner" claim. For example, a "Cheese Dinner," with 25% cheese, would not be feasible or economical to produce, but either a "Beef Dinner for Dogs" or "Chicken Formula Cat Food" could include a side burst "with cheese" if at least 3% cheese is added. Recent amendments to the AAFCO model regulations now allow use of the term "with" as part of the product name, too, such as "Dog Food With Beef" or "Cat Food With Chicken." Now, even a minor change in the wording of the name has a dramatic impact on the minimum amount of the named ingredient required, e.g., a can of "Cat Food With Tuna" could be confused with a can of "Tuna Cat Food," but, whereas the latter example must contain at least 95% tuna, the first needs only 3%. Therefore, the consumer must read labels carefully before purchase to ensure that the desired product is obtained.

Under the "flavor" rule, a specific percentage is not required, but a product must contain an amount sufficient to be able to be detected. There are specific test methods, using animals trained to prefer specific flavors, that can be used to confirm this claim. In the example of "Beef Flavor Dog Food," the word "flavor" must appear on the label in the same size, style and color as the word "beef." The corresponding ingredient may be beef, but more often it is another substance that will give the characterizing flavor, such as beef meal or beef by-products.

With respect to flavors, pet foods often contain "digests," which are materials treated with heat, enzymes and/or acids to form concentrated natural flavors. Only a small amount of a "chicken digest" is needed to produce a "Chicken Flavored Cat Food," even though no actual chicken is added to the food. Stocks or broths are also occasionally added. Whey is often used to add a milk flavor. Often labels will bear a claim of "no artificial flavors." Actually, artificial flavors are rarely used in pet foods. The major exception to that would be artificial smoke or bacon flavors, which are added to some treats.

Dr. Greg Martinez, DVM, graduated from UC Davis, School of Veterinary Medicine in 1980 and has been serving the veterinary needs of Gilroy, California, and Santa Clara Valley ever since. He is a partner/owner in the Gilroy Veterinary Hospital. Greg and Lonna have been married for 32 years. While the couple has no children, at any given time they are parents to at least three dogs and three cats. Greg is an active outdoorsman and nature enthusiast. He likes to hike and swim. He's also an advocate of lifelong learning and an eager student himself.

CPSIA information can be obtained at www.ICGtesting.com
Printed in the USA
244491LV00003B/67/P